Table of Contents

(Answer Key in Back)

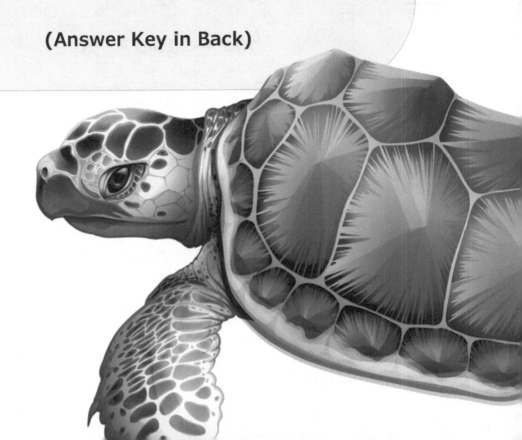

Name: _____

Score:

Problems 1-10: *Fill in the blank.*

① **86 =** _8_ tens and _6_ ones

② **49 =** ___ tens and ___ ones

③ **11 =** ___ tens and ___ ones

④ **8 =** ___ tens and ___ ones

⑤ **27 =** ___ tens and ___ ones

⑥ **93 =** ___ tens and ___ ones

⑦ **35 =** ___ tens and ___ ones

⑧ **77 =** ___ tens and ___ ones

⑨ **54 =** ___ tens and ___ ones

⑩ **60 =** ___ tens and ___ ones

Problems 11-20: *Round each underlined number to the nearest ten. Circle the correct answer.*

(Digits 0-4)   (Digits 5-9)

Round Down   *or*   **Round Up**

⑪ 70 ← **73** → 80

⑫ 40 ← **41** → 50

⑬ 30 ← **39** → 40

⑭ 10 ← **15** → 20

⑮ 60 ← **62** → 70

⑯ 80 ← **88** → 90

⑰ 20 ← **24** → 30

⑱ 0 ← **7** → 10

⑲ 90 ← **92** → 100

⑳ 50 ← **50** → 60

© Libro Studio LLC 2020

Name: _____

Score:

Problems 1-10: *What is the value of the underlined digit?*

① **4̲5** _40_

② **9̲6̲** _6_

③ **5̲8̲** _____

④ **8̲5** _____

⑤ **7̲0̲** _____

⑥ **2̲8** _____

⑦ **4̲7̲** _____

⑧ **1̲6̲** _____

⑨ **3̲0̲** _____

⑩ **9̲5** _____

Problems 11-20: *Write each number in expanded form.*

⑪ 45 = _40 + 5_

⑫ 27 = _____

⑬ 51 = _____

⑭ 90 = _____

⑮ 36 = _____

⑯ 18 = _____

⑰ 60 = _____

⑱ 73 = _____

⑲ 5 = _____

⑳ 84 = _____

Problems 21-30: *Write each number in standard form.*

㉑ 70 + 9 = _79_

㉒ 50 + 3 = _____

㉓ 80 + 5 = _____

㉔ 10 + 2 = _____

㉕ 60 + 6 = _____

㉖ 20 + 1 = _____

㉗ 90 + 0 = _____

㉘ 40 + 8 = _____

㉙ 30 + 4 = _____

㉚ 10 + 6 = _____

© Libro Studio LLC 2020

¼ % 5.3 ✗ 3.107 290 = ∞ ⅄

Name: _____

Score:

Problems 1-5: *Round each underlined number to the nearest ten. Circle the correct answer.*

(Digits 0-4)   (Digits 5-9)

Round Down   or   **Round Up**

① 70 ← **79** → 80

② 40 ← **46** → 50

③ 30 ← **31** → 40

④ 10 ← **13** → 20

⑤ 60 ← **65** → 70

Problems 6-15: *Fill in the blanks, then round each underlined number to the nearest ten. Circle the correct answer.*

Round Down   or   **Round Up**

⑥ _____ ← **12** → _____

⑦ _____ ← **28** → _____

⑧ _____ ← **80** → _____

⑨ _____ ← **92** → _____

⑩ _____ ← **85** → _____

⑪ _____ ← **88** → _____

⑫ _____ ← **24** → _____

⑬ _____ ← **17** → _____

⑭ _____ ← **93** → _____

⑮ _____ ← **50** → _____

© Libro Studio LLC 2020

Name: _____

Score:

Problems 1-20: *Round each number to the nearest ten.*

① 52   ② 83   ③ 29   ④ 25   ⑤ 4

⑥ 91   ⑦ 60   ⑧ 16   ⑨ 77   ⑩ 95

⑪ 43   ⑫ 11   ⑬ 30   ⑭ 6   ⑮ 24

⑯ 78   ⑰ 49   ⑱ 87   ⑲ 64   ⑳ 51

Take a Break
Check Your Work

Problems 21-40: *Round each number to the nearest ten.*

㉑ 80   ㉒ 3   ㉓ 15   ㉔ 25   ㉕ 76

㉖ 49   ㉗ 55   ㉘ 38   ㉙ 20   ㉚ 17

㉛ 97   ㉜ 64   ㉝ 12   ㉞ 86   ㉟ 31

㊱ 54   ㊲ 67   ㊳ 28   ㊴ 93   ㊵ 7

© Libro Studio LLC 2020

Day 5
Tens Place

Name: _____

Score:

Problems 1-10: *Round each number to the nearest ten.*

① 37　　② 18　　③ 72　　④ 85　　⑤ 40

⑥ 59　　⑦ 96　　⑧ 12　　⑨ 5　　⑩ 21

Problems 11-30: *Round each number to the nearest ten, then add.*

⑪ 10 + 47　　⑫ 32 + 59　　⑬ 48 + 17　　⑭ 55 + 30

⑮ 96 + 11　　⑯ 42 + 41　　⑰ 18 + 74　　⑱ 69 + 97

⑲ 66 + 67　　⑳ 15 + 16　　㉑ 43 + 23　　㉒ 19 + 49

㉓ 70 + 25　　㉔ 37 + 52　　㉕ 20 + 40　　㉖ 11 + 57

㉗ 56 + 68　　㉘ 71 + 97　　㉙ 23 + 54　　㉚ 36 + 22

© Libro Studio LLC 2020

¼ % 5.3 x 3.107 290 = 8

Name: _____

Score:

Problems 1-5: *Fill in the blanks.*

① **186 =** ____ hundreds, ____ tens, and ____ ones

② **410 =** ____ hundreds, ____ tens, and ____ ones

③ **723 =** ____ hundreds, ____ tens, and ____ ones

④ **905 =** ____ hundreds, ____ tens, and ____ ones

⑤ **97 =** ____ hundreds, ____ tens, and ____ ones

Problems 6-15: *Round each underlined number to the nearest hundred. Circle the correct answer.*

(Digits 0-4)　　　　　　　　(Digits 5-9)

Round Down　　　*or*　　　**Round Up**

⑥　　600 ← **677** → 700

⑦　　100 ← **180** → 200

⑧　　400 ← **429** → 500

⑨　　300 ← **305** → 400

⑩　　0 ← **99** → 100

⑪　　200 ← **261** → 300

⑫　　800 ← **847** → 900

⑬　　500 ← **513** → 600

⑭　　900 ← **952** → 1,000

⑮　　0 ← **38** → 100

© Libro Studio LLC 2020

Name: _____

Score:

Problems 1-10: *What is the value of the underlined digit?*

① **4̲17** *400*

② **256̲** _____

③ **68̲3** _____

④ **8̲40** _____

⑤ **50̲5** _____

⑥ **12̲8** _____

⑦ **7̲99** _____

⑧ **56̲5** _____

⑨ **307̲** _____

⑩ **9̲52** _____

Problems 11-20: *Write each number in expanded form.*

⑪ **365 =** *300 + 60 + 5*

⑫ **427 =** _____

⑬ **689 =** _____

⑭ **164 =** _____

⑮ **853 =** _____

⑯ **572 =** _____

⑰ **931 =** _____

⑱ **208 =** _____

⑲ **450 =** _____

⑳ **797 =** _____

Problems 21-30: *Write each number in standard form.*

㉑ **600 + 70 + 9 =** *679*

㉒ **700 + 10 + 2 =** _____

㉓ **100 + 50 + 5 =** _____

㉔ **400 + 3 =** _____

㉕ **300 + 90 + 1 =** _____

㉖ **500 + 80 =** _____

㉗ **200 + 30 + 6 =** _____

㉘ **900 + 70 + 4 =** _____

㉙ **100 + 10 + 1 =** _____

㉚ **400 + 80 + 9 =** _____

© Libro Studio LLC 2020

Name: _____

Score:

Problems 1-5: *Round each underlined number to the nearest hundred. Circle the correct answer.*

(Digits 0-4)		(Digits 5-9)
Round Down	*or*	**Round Up**

①   900 ← **932** → 1,000

②   500 ← **513** → 600

③   200 ← **250** → 300

④   600 ← **674** → 700

⑤   0 ← **82** → 100

Problems 6-15: *Fill in the blanks, then round each underlined number to the nearest hundred. Circle the correct answer.*

Round Down	*or*	**Round Up**

⑥   _____ ← **661** → _____

⑦   _____ ← **190** → _____

⑧   _____ ← **47** → _____

⑨   _____ ← **838** → _____

⑩   _____ ← **245** → _____

⑪   _____ ← **455** → _____

⑫   _____ ← **973** → _____

⑬   _____ ← **62** → _____

⑭   _____ ← **917** → _____

⑮   _____ ← **335** → _____

© Libro Studio LLC 2020

Name: _____

Score:

Problems 1-20: *Round each number to the nearest hundred.*

① 512   ② 383   ③ 729   ④ 125   ⑤ 354

⑥ 291   ⑦ 760   ⑧ 416   ⑨ 837   ⑩ 975

⑪ 133   ⑫ 741   ⑬ 922   ⑭ 63   ⑮ 571

⑯ 228   ⑰ 462   ⑱ 187   ⑲ 364   ⑳ 751

Take a Break
Check Your Work

Problems 21-40: *Round each number to the nearest hundred.*

㉑ 522   ㉒ 724   ㉓ 839   ㉔ 163   ㉕ 325

㉖ 741   ㉗ 405   ㉘ 236   ㉙ 610   ㉚ 147

㉛ 953   ㉜ 571   ㉝ 922   ㉞ 741   ㉟ 518

㊱ 482   ㊲ 261   ㊳ 149   ㊴ 342   ㊵ 644

© Libro Studio LLC 2020

Name: _____

Score:

Problems 1-10: *Round each number to the nearest hundred.*

① 156　　② 513　　③ 866　　④ 29　　⑤ 947

⑥ 305　　⑦ 71　　⑧ 280　　⑨ 400　　⑩ 694

Problems 11-30: *Round each number to the nearest hundred, then add.*

⑪ 258 + 147　　⑫ 369 + 581　　⑬ 470 + 692　　⑭ 925 + 814

⑮ 741 + 963　　⑯ 296 + 529　　⑰ 852 + 185　　⑱ 418 + 630

⑲ 371 + 593　　⑳ 159 + 604　　㉑ 482 + 715　　㉒ 826 + 937

㉓ 406 + 840　　㉔ 951 + 517　　㉕ 628 + 284　　㉖ 739 + 395

㉗ 161 + 949　　㉘ 616 + 727　　㉙ 272 + 838　　㉚ 494 + 383

© Libro Studio LLC 2020

Name: _____

Score:

Problems 1-10: *Round each underlined number to the nearest <u>ten</u>. Circle the correct answer.*

| (Digits 0-4) | | (Digits 5-9) |
| **Round Down** | *or* | **Round Up** |

①   670 ← **677** → 680

②   180 ← **184** → 190

③   420 ← **429** → 430

④   390 ← **395** → 400

⑤   90 ← **99** → 100

⑥   260 ← **261** → 370

⑦   840 ← **847** → 850

⑧   510 ← **513** → 520

⑨   950 ← **952** → 960

⑩   30 ← **38** → 40

Problems 11-20: *Round each number to the nearest <u>ten</u>.*

⑪ **83**   ⑫ **375**   ⑬ **652**   ⑭ **116**   ⑮ **597**

⑯ **708**   ⑰ **229**   ⑱ **901**   ⑲ **465**   ⑳ **684**

© Libro Studio LLC 2020

Name: _____

Problems 1-15: *Round each number to the nearest hundred, then to the nearest ten.*

		Nearest Hundred	Nearest Ten
①	186	_____	_____
②	410	_____	_____
③	723	_____	_____
④	905	_____	_____
⑤	87	_____	_____
⑥	349	_____	_____
⑦	883	_____	_____
⑧	200	_____	_____
⑨	557	_____	_____
⑩	104	_____	_____
⑪	648	_____	_____
⑫	961	_____	_____
⑬	25	_____	_____
⑭	319	_____	_____
⑮	795	_____	_____

© Libro Studio LLC 2020

Problems 1-12: *Round each number to the nearest <u>hundred</u>, then add.*

① 720 + 407   ② 283 + 516   ③ 834 + 396   ④ 618 + 940

⑤ 408 + 162   ⑥ 620 + 399   ⑦ 285 + 841   ⑧ 514 + 731

⑨ 306 + 742   ⑩ 528 + 295   ⑪ 854 + 419   ⑫ 631 + 964

Problems 13-24: *Round each number to the nearest <u>ten</u>, then add.*

⑬ 813 + 257   ⑭ 148 + 479   ⑮ 580 + 703   ⑯ 367 + 691

⑰ 197 + 531   ⑱ 753 + 209   ⑲ 864 + 642   ⑳ 319 + 421

㉑ 913 + 246   ㉒ 688 + 802   ㉓ 701 + 570   ㉔ 357 + 468

© Libro Studio LLC 2020

Name: _____

Score:

Problems 1-5: *Fill in the blanks.*

①   **3,016 =** ____ thousands, ____ hundreds, ____ tens, and ____ ones

②   **9,425 =** ____ thousands, ____ hundreds, ____ tens, and ____ ones

③   **7,178 =** ____ thousands, ____ hundreds, ____ tens, and ____ ones

④   **5,905 =** ____ thousands, ____ hundreds, ____ tens, and ____ ones

⑤   **1,237 =** ____ thousands, ____ hundreds, ____ tens, and ____ ones

Problems 6-15: *Round each underlined number to the nearest thousand. Circle the correct answer.*

(Digits 0-4)		(Digits 5-9)
Round Down	*or*	**Round Up**

⑥   1,000 ← **1,392** → 2,000

⑦   8,000 ← **8,014** → 9,000

⑧   2,000 ← **2,495** → 3,000

⑨   5,000 ← **5,630** → 6,000

⑩   0 ← **671** → 1,000

⑪   3,000 ← **3,813** → 4,000

⑫   7,000 ← **7,189** → 8,000

⑬   4,000 ← **4,255** → 5,000

⑭   0 ← **368** → 1,000

⑮   9,000 ← **9,500** → 10,000

© Libro Studio LLC 2020

Name: _____

Score:

Problems 1-10: *What is the value of the underlined digit?*

① **4564** _4,000_

② **9652** _____

③ **5813** _____

④ **8584** _____

⑤ **7091** _____

⑥ **2860** _____

⑦ **4718** _____

⑧ **1627** _____

⑨ **3069** _____

⑩ **9547** _____

Problems 11-15: *Write each number in expanded form.*

⑪ **1,835 =** _1,000 + 800 + 30 + 5_

⑫ **5,821 =** _____

⑬ **7,462 =** _____

⑭ **3,990 =** _____

⑮ **6,045 =** _____

Problems 16-20: *Write each number in standard form.*

⑯ **6,000 + 400 + 60 + 3 =** _____

⑰ **1,000 + 500 + 20 + 7 =** _____

⑱ **3,000 + 90 + 9 =** _____

⑲ **7,000 + 200 + 80 + 4 =** _____

⑳ **9,000 + 400 =** _____

© Libro Studio LLC 2020

Name: _____

Score:

Problems 1-5: *Round each underlined number to the nearest thousand. Circle the correct answer.*

(Digits 0-4)   (Digits 5-9)

Round Down   or   **Round Up**

①   7,000 ← **7,139** → 8,000

②   6,000 ← **6,483** → 7,000

③   1,000 ← **1,522** → 2,000

④   9,000 ← **9,704** → 10,000

⑤   3,000 ← **3,095** → 4,000

Problems 6-15: *Fill in the blanks, then round each underlined number to the nearest thousand. Circle the correct answer.*

Round Down   or   **Round Up**

⑥   _____ ← **3,168** → _____

⑦   _____ ← **458** → _____

⑧   _____ ← **6,621** → _____

⑨   _____ ← **8,385** → _____

⑩   _____ ← **4,833** → _____

⑪   _____ ← **1,496** → _____

⑫   _____ ← **5,067** → _____

⑬   _____ ← **7,582** → _____

⑭   _____ ← **617** → _____

⑮   _____ ← **2,935** → _____

© Libro Studio LLC 2020

Name: _____

Score:

Problems 1-20: *Round each number to the nearest thousand.*

① 1,357   ② 7,913   ③ 3,579   ④ 9,135   ⑤ 5,791

⑥ 2,468   ⑦ 8,024   ⑧ 4,680   ⑨ 6,802   ⑩ 1,470

⑪ 2,086   ⑫ 3,197   ⑬ 4,208   ⑭ 5,319   ⑮ 6,420

⑯ 7,531   ⑰ 2,581   ⑱ 8,642   ⑲ 9,754   ⑳ 1,471

Take a Break
Check Your Work

Problems 21-40: *Round each number to the nearest thousand.*

㉑ 3,074   ㉒ 4,703   ㉓ 5,814   ㉔ 6,925   ㉕ 7,036

㉖ 8,147   ㉗ 9,258   ㉘ 1,593   ㉙ 3,715   ㉚ 2,604

㉛ 4,826   ㉜ 8,260   ㉝ 5,937   ㉞ 7,459   ㉟ 6,048

㊱ 9,771   ㊲ 4,062   ㊳ 1,839   ㊴ 2,340   ㊵ 3,951

© Libro Studio LLC 2020

Name: _____

Score:

Problems 1-10: *Round each number to the nearest thousand.*

① 3,296 ② 5,713 ③ 7,866 ④ 9,629 ⑤ 2,047

⑥ 4,605 ⑦ 1,145 ⑧ 6,356 ⑨ 8,924 ⑩ 694

Problems 11-25: *Round each number to the nearest thousand, then add.*

⑪ 5,173 + 1,616 ⑫ 8,406 + 6,284 ⑬ 9,517 + 7,395

⑭ 7,272 + 5,050 ⑮ 2,727 + 6,161 ⑯ 4,050 + 3,838

⑰ 4,274 + 1,738 ⑱ 3,975 + 9,494 ⑲ 2,841 + 8,383

⑳ 5,296 + 8,529 ㉑ 1,970 + 6,584 ㉒ 9,630 + 7,418

㉓ 2,281 + 7,836 ㉔ 5,514 + 3692 ㉕ 4,403 + 5,514

© Libro Studio LLC 2020

Name: _____

Score:

Problems 1-15: *Round each number to the:*

		Nearest Thousand	Nearest Hundred	Nearest Ten
①	**6,301**	_____	_____	_____
②	**1,453**	_____	_____	_____
③	**8,905**	_____	_____	_____
④	**4,258**	_____	_____	_____
⑤	**6,523**	_____	_____	_____
⑥	**2,886**	_____	_____	_____
⑦	**5,705**	_____	_____	_____
⑧	**1,972**	_____	_____	_____
⑨	**3,530**	_____	_____	_____
⑩	**2,461**	_____	_____	_____
⑪	**9,642**	_____	_____	_____
⑫	**3,897**	_____	_____	_____
⑬	**5,316**	_____	_____	_____
⑭	**3,497**	_____	_____	_____
⑮	**7,098**	_____	_____	_____

© Libro Studio LLC 2020

Day 20
Mixed Rounding

Name: _____

Score:

Problems 1-20: *Round each number to the nearest <u>thousand</u>.*

① 2,471   ② 4,321   ③ 6,789   ④ 8,901   ⑤ 2,109

⑥ 1,987   ⑦ 3,210   ⑧ 5,678   ⑨ 9,012   ⑩ 1,259

⑪ 8,765   ⑫ 1,248   ⑬ 6,543   ⑭ 2,345   ⑮ 7,890

⑯ 4,567   ⑰ 9,765   ⑱ 3,456   ⑲ 7,654   ⑳ 5,132

Take a Break
Check Your Work

Problems 21-40: *Round each number to the nearest <u>hundred</u>.*

㉑ 2,976   ㉒ 2,741   ㉓ 5,063   ㉔ 7,926   ㉕ 1,506

㉖ 8,407   ㉗ 4,693   ㉘ 6,493   ㉙ 3,841   ㉚ 9,149

㉛ 1,250   ㉜ 3,101   ㉝ 1,360   ㉞ 4,693   ㉟ 5,063

㊱ 6,435   ㊲ 7,049   ㊳ 2,730   ㊴ 9,953   ㊵ 8,419

© Libro Studio LLC 2020

Day 21
Mixed Rounding

Name: _____

Score:

Problems 1-15: *Round each number to the:*

		Nearest Thousand	Nearest Hundred	Nearest Ten
①	9,420	_____	_____	_____
②	6,591	_____	_____	_____
③	1,078	_____	_____	_____
④	4,353	_____	_____	_____
⑤	5,984	_____	_____	_____
⑥	2,846	_____	_____	_____
⑦	4,072	_____	_____	_____
⑧	1,337	_____	_____	_____
⑨	3,250	_____	_____	_____
⑩	6,695	_____	_____	_____
⑪	5,418	_____	_____	_____
⑫	8,905	_____	_____	_____
⑬	2,181	_____	_____	_____
⑭	7,020	_____	_____	_____
⑮	3,589	_____	_____	_____

© Libro Studio LLC 2020

Name: _____

Score:

Problems 1-20: *Round each number to the nearest thousand.*

① 3,527 ② 8,372 ③ 1,061 ④ 9,805 ⑤ 4,607

⑥ 2,780 ⑦ 7,586 ⑧ 4,039 ⑨ 5,278 ⑩ 9,713

⑪ 7,602 ⑫ 1,402 ⑬ 6,726 ⑭ 8,534 ⑮ 7,262

⑯ 8,953 ⑰ 5,031 ⑱ 2,847 ⑲ 6,317 ⑳ 3,814

Take a Break
Check Your Work

Problems 21-40: *Round each number to the nearest hundred.*

㉑ 1,579 ㉒ 5,986 ㉓ 9,640 ㉔ 4,159 ㉕ 9,418

㉖ 1,263 ㉗ 2,584 ㉘ 3,851 ㉙ 8,009 ㉚ 4,790

㉛ 9,710 ㉜ 5,267 ㉝ 1,306 ㉞ 6,139 ㉟ 6,752

㊱ 8,367 ㊲ 7,283 ㊳ 3,918 ㊴ 7,925 ㊵ 2,570

© Libro Studio LLC 2020

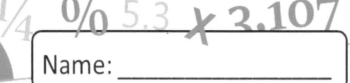

Name: _____

Score:

Problems 1-15: *Round each number to the:*

		Nearest Thousand	Nearest Hundred	Nearest Ten
①	6,387	_____	_____	_____
②	2,601	_____	_____	_____
③	1,099	_____	_____	_____
④	5,304	_____	_____	_____
⑤	7,438	_____	_____	_____
⑥	9,727	_____	_____	_____
⑦	4,976	_____	_____	_____
⑧	6,813	_____	_____	_____
⑨	5,720	_____	_____	_____
⑩	4,089	_____	_____	_____
⑪	2,496	_____	_____	_____
⑫	7,255	_____	_____	_____
⑬	3,814	_____	_____	_____
⑭	8,347	_____	_____	_____
⑮	3,128	_____	_____	_____

© Libro Studio LLC 2020

Day 24
Mixed Rounding

Score:

Problems 1-20: *Round each number to the nearest <u>thousand</u>.*

① 9,164   ② 4,619   ③ 8,524   ④ 3,452   ⑤ 2,370

⑥ 6,892   ⑦ 2,037   ⑧ 7,294   ⑨ 3,159   ⑩ 7,026

⑪ 1,793   ⑫ 9,451   ⑬ 5,691   ⑭ 1,887   ⑮ 6,370

⑯ 8,754   ⑰ 8,217   ⑱ 4,093   ⑲ 9,571   ⑳ 5,927

Take a Break
Check Your Work

Problems 21-40: *Round each number to the nearest <u>hundred</u>.*

㉑ 2,637   ㉒ 6,381   ㉓ 1,018   ㉔ 5,891   ㉕ 4,169

㉖ 2,944   ㉗ 2,258   ㉘ 3,965   ㉙ 8,012   ㉚ 9,526

㉛ 7,874   ㉜ 7,265   ㉝ 1,695   ㉞ 4,901   ㉟ 5,218

㊱ 8,259   ㊲ 3,186   ㊳ 6,913   ㊴ 9,631   ㊵ 1,846

© Libro Studio LLC 2020

Name: _____

Score:

Problems 1-9: *Round each number to the nearest <u>thousand</u>, then add.*

① 7,321 + 9,784

② 1,630 + 5,206

③ 4,975 + 9,142

④ 8,471 + 3,928

⑤ 4,315 + 2,036

⑥ 8,892 + 5,685

⑦ 1,562 + 3,110

⑧ 6,785 + 6,617

⑨ 4,975 + 2,417

Problems 10-18: *Round each number to the nearest <u>hundred</u>, then add.*

⑩ 4,206 + 1,876

⑪ 8,140 + 9,712

⑫ 3,089 + 7,326

⑬ 9,254 + 5,936

⑭ 1,208 + 3,194

⑮ 6,471 + 2,348

⑯ 7,969 + 2,791

⑰ 8,110 + 5,832

⑱ 4,443 + 6,482

© Libro Studio LLC 2020

Name: _____

Score:

Problems 1-9: *Round each number to the nearest <u>thousand</u>, then add.*

① 3,287 + 1,846   ② 8,135 + 9,006   ③ 6,571 + 7,496

④ 2,374 + 4,730   ⑤ 5,416 + 5,638   ⑥ 9,756 + 2,379

⑦ 3,892 + 4,310   ⑧ 6,914 + 8,122   ⑨ 1,561 + 7,603

Problems 10-18: *Round each number to the nearest <u>hundred</u>, then add.*

⑩ 1,549 + 2,106   ⑪ 6,663 + 9,483   ⑫ 4,331 + 3,795

⑬ 5,700 + 8,327   ⑭ 7,284 + 4,752   ⑮ 8,074 + 3,297

⑯ 2,688 + 6,259   ⑰ 5,840 + 1,862   ⑱ 7,901 + 9,439

© Libro Studio LLC 2020

Name: _____

Score:

Problems 1-9: *Round each number to the nearest <u>thousand</u>, then subtract.*

① 6,795 – 2,080 ② 4,871 – 3,103 ③ 9,391 – 2,999

④ 5,212 – 4,368 ⑤ 9,535 – 1,607 ⑥ 6,688 – 3,164

⑦ 8,654 – 7,227 ⑧ 7,624 – 1,893 ⑨ 8,036 – 5,917

Problems 10-18: *Round each number to the nearest <u>hundred</u>, then subtract.*

⑩ 4,374 – 2,318 ⑪ 7,281 – 1,825 ⑫ 3,919 – 2,509

⑬ 9,823 – 5,862 ⑭ 4,750 – 1,396 ⑮ 8,436 – 7,543

⑯ 8,127 – 6,887 ⑰ 9,673 – 6,111 ⑱ 5,681 – 3,465

© Libro Studio LLC 2020

Day 28
Mixed Rounding

Name: _____

Score:

Problems 1-9: *Round each number to the nearest <u>thousand</u>, then subtract.*

① 5,806 – 2,463

② 3,128 – 1,603

③ 8,553 – 4,312

④ 5,460 – 3,087

⑤ 9,555 – 8,941

⑥ 7,231 – 4,473

⑦ 9,670 – 6,209

⑧ 2,314 – 1,009

⑨ 7,428 – 6,941

Problems 10-18: *Round each number to the nearest <u>hundred</u>, then subtract.*

⑩ 5,326 – 2,445

⑪ 2,818 – 1,678

⑫ 9,306 – 8,899

⑬ 7,214 – 1,237

⑭ 5,280 – 3,063

⑮ 4,179 – 3,646

⑯ 6,702 – 6,358

⑰ 9,134 – 4,897

⑱ 8,779 – 7,923

© Libro Studio LLC 2020

Name: _____

Score:

Problems 1-12: *Round each number to the nearest <u>thousand</u>, then add.*

① 6,019 + 6,532 + 3,916

② 9,655 + 4,123 + 1,973

③ 3,630 + 9,436 + 6,703

④ 3,316 + 9,762 + 6,018

⑤ 4,198 + 1,471 + 7,954

⑥ 4,836 + 1,303 + 7,516

⑦ 5,026 + 2,312 + 8,291

⑧ 5,212 + 2,615 + 8,831

⑨ 3,730 + 9,941 + 7,642

⑩ 4,875 + 1,096 + 7,217

⑪ 8,132 + 5,777 + 2,338

⑫ 8,310 + 5,472 + 2,616

© Libro Studio LLC 2020

Name: _____

Score:

Problems 1-12: *Round each number to the nearest <u>thousand</u>, then add.*

① 1,504 + 7,716 + 4,018

② 2,489 + 8,238 + 5,362

③ 4,911 + 1,830 + 7,012

④ 8,755 + 2,489 + 5,963

⑤ 6,289 + 9,354 + 9,157

⑥ 3,012 + 3,801 + 6,733

⑦ 2,853 + 8,490 + 2,629

⑧ 5,065 + 4,362 + 6,721

⑨ 1,006 + 3,976 + 7,212

⑩ 4,186 + 5,312 + 6,206

⑪ 7,303 + 1,687 + 9,064

⑫ 8,538 + 3,853 + 9,909

© Libro Studio LLC 2020

Name: _____

Score:

Problems 1-15: *Write the value of each underlined digit in number form and written form. Refer to the back of the book for the names of these place values.*

		Number Form:	**Written Form:**

① **3,046,875** *40,000* *forty thousand*

② **9,825,417** _____ _____

③ **8,178,044** _____ _____

④ **4,985,652** _____ _____

⑤ **2,158,276** _____ _____

⑥ **7,516,290** _____ _____

⑦ **1,681,259** _____ _____

⑧ **6,395,104** _____ _____

⑨ **8,067,235** _____ _____

⑩ **1,678,342** _____ _____

⑪ **5,806,213** _____ _____

⑫ **4,158,947** _____ _____

⑬ **2,560,178** _____ _____

⑭ **3,967,341** _____ _____

⑮ **9,780,216** _____ _____

© Libro Studio LLC 2020

Name: _____

Score:

Problems 1-15: *Write the value of each written number in standard form.*

Standard Form:

① Six million, three hundred five thousand, four hundred seventy-two = <u>6,305,472</u>

② Two million, four hundred sixty-seven thousand, nine hundred thirty-one = _____

③ Nine million, seventy-eight thousand, six hundred twenty-four = _____

④ One million, nine hundred twenty-eight thousand, six hundred fifty-three = _____

⑤ Seven million, one hundred twenty-three thousand, four hundred eighty = _____

⑥ Five million, Two hundred seventy thousand, six hundred eighty-nine = _____

⑦ Three million, five hundred twenty-eight thousand, seven hundred six = _____

⑧ Six million, eight hundred ninety-two thousand, three hundred seven-ten = _____

⑨ One million, eight hundred sixty-two thousand, nine hundred fifty = _____

⑩ Four million, eight hundred twenty thousand, one hundred seventy-five = _____

⑪ Seven million, three hundred eighty-four thousand, five hundred seventy = _____

⑫ Two million, seven hundred thirty-four thousand, five hundred ninety = _____

⑬ Nine million, one hundred twenty thousand, three hundred sixty-eight = _____

⑭ Eight million, seven hundred ninety-five thousand, six hundred fifty-two = _____

⑮ Eight million, six hundred fifty-four thousand, two hundred thirty-one = _____

© Libro Studio LLC 2020

Name: _____

Score:

Problems 1-12: *Write the value of each number in written form.*

① 1,629,170 = _One million, six hundred twenty-nine thousand,_
one hundred seventy

② 1,489,637 = _____

③ 3,072,136 = _____

④ 8,523,674 = _____

⑤ 4,673,950 = _____

⑥ 9,700,613 = _____

⑦ 6,839,215 = _____

⑧ 5,342,967 = _____

⑨ 3,206,591 = _____

⑩ 4,732,815 = _____

⑪ 2,154,789 = _____

⑫ 7,012,378 = _____

© Libro Studio LLC 2020

Name: _____

Score:

Problems 1-15: *Round each number to the nearest:*

		Million	Hundred Thousand	Ten Thousand
①	9,043,857	_____	_____	_____
②	6,532,567	_____	_____	_____
③	7,410,892	_____	_____	_____
④	3,675,438	_____	_____	_____
⑤	1,867,543	_____	_____	_____
⑥	9,654,321	_____	_____	_____
⑦	4,243,078	_____	_____	_____
⑧	6,889,017	_____	_____	_____
⑨	2,036,789	_____	_____	_____
⑩	5,721,064	_____	_____	_____
⑪	7,936,150	_____	_____	_____
⑫	3,458,791	_____	_____	_____
⑬	4,602,194	_____	_____	_____
⑭	8,390,276	_____	_____	_____
⑮	5,185,826	_____	_____	_____

© Libro Studio LLC 2020

Problems 1-16: *Round each number to the nearest __million__.*

① 3,921,067 ② 9,360,218 ③ 6,031,781 ④ 3,791,864

⑤ 2,860,395 ⑥ 8,189,217 ⑦ 1,534,672 ⑧ 9,627,843

⑨ 5,203,689 ⑩ 8,791,345 ⑪ 4,407,683 ⑫ 1,652,870

⑬ 5,196,462 ⑭ 2,376,406 ⑮ 7,869,123 ⑯ 4,782,176

Take a Break
Check Your Work

Problems 17-32: *Round each number to the nearest __hundred thousand__.*

⑰ 6,754,310 ⑱ 1,380,672 ⑲ 5,821,367 ⑳ 8,106,734

㉑ 7,641,539 ㉒ 4,639,125 ㉓ 7,071,926 ㉔ 2,987,651

㉕ 1,367,925 ㉖ 9,321,678 ㉗ 6,351,829 ㉘ 3,037,214

㉙ 9,542,381 ㉚ 2,493,671 ㉛ 3,724,568 ㉜ 8,264,138

© Libro Studio LLC 2020

Name: _____

Score:

Problems 1-15: *Round each number to the nearest:*

		Million	Hundred Thousand	Ten Thousand
①	9,043,857	_____	_____	_____
②	8,860,671	_____	_____	_____
③	6,315,294	_____	_____	_____
④	1,749,326	_____	_____	_____
⑤	4,923,601	_____	_____	_____
⑥	5,071,468	_____	_____	_____
⑦	7,429,863	_____	_____	_____
⑧	2,608,953	_____	_____	_____
⑨	5,234,689	_____	_____	_____
⑩	6,570,190	_____	_____	_____
⑪	3,612,987	_____	_____	_____
⑫	9,406,215	_____	_____	_____
⑬	7,187,642	_____	_____	_____
⑭	4,365,719	_____	_____	_____
⑮	8,579,300	_____	_____	_____

© Libro Studio LLC 2020

Name: _____

Score:

Problems 1-16: *Round each number to the nearest <u>million</u>.*

① 1,234,567 ② 9,721,345 ③ 3,126,879 ④ 6,423,018

⑤ 9,837,653 ⑥ 3,609,815 ⑦ 5,762,834 ⑧ 1,648,210

⑨ 2,095,432 ⑩ 4,286,751 ⑪ 7,436,887 ⑫ 4,503,861

⑬ 5,862,134 ⑭ 8,302,176 ⑮ 2,974,334 ⑯ 3,587,623

Take a Break
Check Your Work

Problems 17-32: *Round each number to the nearest <u>hundred thousand</u>.*

⑰ 4,436,325 ⑱ 8,682,455 ⑲ 1,514,897 ⑳ 3,656,928

㉑ 9,996,666 ㉒ 5,771,230 ㉓ 6,342,912 ㉔ 6,182,907

㉕ 3,210,063 ㉖ 1,878,029 ㉗ 7,091,926 ㉘ 2,428,866

㉙ 8,736,541 ㉚ 9,317,163 ㉛ 2,986,644 ㉜ 7,286,543

© Libro Studio LLC 2020

Name: _____

Score:

Problems 1-15: *Round each number to the nearest:*

		Million	Hundred Thousand	Ten Thousand
①	9,043,857	_____	_____	_____
②	6,928,311	_____	_____	_____
③	1,739,645	_____	_____	_____
④	5,192,831	_____	_____	_____
⑤	7,005,432	_____	_____	_____
⑥	2,679,430	_____	_____	_____
⑦	6,334,597	_____	_____	_____
⑧	4,743,287	_____	_____	_____
⑨	8,369,428	_____	_____	_____
⑩	3,295,806	_____	_____	_____
⑪	7,801,000	_____	_____	_____
⑫	5,162,389	_____	_____	_____
⑬	9,554,194	_____	_____	_____
⑭	4,428,210	_____	_____	_____
⑮	8,365,499	_____	_____	_____

© Libro Studio LLC 2020

Name: _____

Score:

Problems 1-6: *Round each number to the nearest <u>million</u>, then add.*

① **2,643,508 + 8,467,255**

② **5,342,144 + 2,897,856**

③ **9,096,832 + 3,776,653**

④ **6,528,741 + 9,156,407**

⑤ **1,678,234 + 4,289,639**

⑥ **7,802,490 + 1,789,243**

Problems 7-12: *Round each number to the nearest <u>hundred thousand</u>, then add.*

⑦ **5,649,107+ 1,802,456**

⑧ **7,936,451 + 3,778,822**

⑨ **2,513,469 + 8,620,317**

⑩ **4,206,813 + 5,989,105**

⑪ **9,765,432 + 3,072,814**

⑫ **6,435,178 + 4,216,788**

© Libro Studio LLC 2020

Name: _____

Score:

Problems 1-6: *Round each number to the nearest <u>million</u>, then add.*

① 8,731,459 + 5,687,317

② 2,279,345 + 8,321,657

③ 6,881,954 + 9,702,536

④ 3,912,072 + 6,321,984

⑤ 7,529,061 + 1,496,328

⑥ 4,582,193 + 7,059,816

Problems 7-12: *Round each number to the nearest <u>hundred thousand</u>, then add.*

⑦ 1,812,465 + 6,573,817

⑧ 2,468,913 + 2,390,642

⑨ 9,946,214 + 5,320,649

⑩ 1,972,315 + 8,106,739

⑪ 4,330,870 + 9,052,288

⑫ 3,715,486 + 7,982,154

© Libro Studio LLC 2020

Day 41
Millions Place

Name: _____

Score:

Problems 1-6: *Round each number to the nearest <u>million</u>, then subtract.*

① **4,148,219 – 1,478,217**

② **3,997,062 – 2,071,631**

③ **8,660,123 – 5,186,214**

④ **9,764,352 – 4,579,111**

⑤ **7,532,816 – 3,302,194**

⑥ **6,912,788 – 5,890,241**

Problems 7-12: *Round each number to the nearest <u>hundred thousand</u>, then subtract.*

⑦ **7,487,010 – 1,954,763**

⑧ **4,046,788 – 2,773,416**

⑨ **5,308,197 – 3,217,489**

⑩ **8,591,068 – 6,621,384**

⑪ **9,566,837 – 8,487,015**

⑫ **7,342,961 – 6,135,420**

© Libro Studio LLC 2020

Name: _____

Score:

Problems 1-6: *Round each number to the nearest <u>million</u>, then subtract.*

① 3,234,021 – 2,710,685

② 7,398,764 – 5,684,327

③ 2,531,021 – 1,467,829

④ 8,615,482 – 1,954,376

⑤ 9,864,787 – 6,059,462

⑥ 9,139,060 – 4,561,238

Problems 7-12: *Round each number to the nearest <u>hundred thousand</u>, then subtract.*

⑦ 8,634,799 – 5,609,135

⑧ 6,951,483 – 3,760,215

⑨ 7,697,200 – 2,526,914

⑩ 9,048,768 – 7,480,126

⑪ 4,218,991 – 3,470,791

⑫ 5,391,784 – 4,256,509

© Libro Studio LLC 2020

Name: _____

Score:

Problems 1-12: *Round each number to the nearest <u>million</u>, then add.*

①
6,222,166
1,830,625
+ 5,067,183

②
9,762,523
5,283,146
+ 1,568,240

③
5,196,724
9,703,217
+ 4,298,653

④
7,440,321
2,675,482
+ 6,325,487

⑤
1,539,781
6,193,217
+ 2,703,145

⑥
6,430,196
1,612,345
+ 5,577,061

⑦
8,201,434
3,710,896
+ 7,926,314

⑧
3,721,483
8,902,010
+ 4,391,267

⑨
2,498,106
7,890,213
+ 3,018,976

⑩
7,601,354
2,760,341
+ 8,191,234

⑪
9,921,860
4,571,239
+ 8,812,675

⑫
4,128,769
9,070,621
+ 3,331,110

© Libro Studio LLC 2020

Name: _____

Score: _____

Problems 1-12: *Round each number to the nearest* <u>million</u>, *then add.*

①   3,702,544
      8,120,654
   + 4,492,083

②   9,018,736
      5,290,631
   + 1,395,487

③   6,721,049
      2,916,754
   + 7,263,145

④   6,810,342
      1,458,717
   + 5,382,168

⑤   9,127,876
      4,860,219
   + 8,452,017

⑥   3,700,214
      7,241,976
   + 2,098,240

⑦   8,197,340
      3,872,164
   + 7,523,651

⑧   2,615,389
      6,010,235
   + 1,972,130

⑨   5,436,127
      9,632,187
   + 4,872,183

⑩   9,302,183
      4,502,917
   + 8,052,109

⑪   3,791,200
      7,164,328
   + 2,563,198

⑫   6,871,239
      1,086,593
   + 5,492,067

© Libro Studio LLC 2020

Name: _____

Score:

Tens	Ones		Tenths	Hundredths	Thousandths
1	5	.	7	8	2

Standard Form = 15.782
Expanded Form = 10 + 5 + 0.7 + 0.08 + 0.002
Written Form = Fifteen and seven hundred eighty-two thousandths

Problems 1-12: *Write the value of each underlined digit in number form and written form.*

		Number Form:	**Written Form:**
①	5.<u>7</u>81	0.7	seven tenths
②	<u>7</u>.346	_____	_____
③	8.13<u>9</u>	_____	_____
④	2.<u>5</u>	_____	_____
⑤	2<u>3</u>.97	_____	_____
⑥	4.08<u>1</u>	_____	_____
⑦	1.3<u>7</u>	_____	_____
⑧	<u>7</u>.2	_____	_____
⑨	<u>5</u>8.006	_____	_____
⑩	0.9<u>5</u>	_____	_____
⑪	<u>6</u>.802	_____	_____
⑫	3.0<u>5</u>	_____	_____

© Libro Studio LLC 2020

Day 46
Decimals

Name: _____

Score: ⬯

Problems 1-15: *Write the value of each written number in standard form.*

Standard Form:

① Sixty-one and twenty-seven thousandths =   _61.027_

② Seventy-five and nine hundred thirty-four thousandths =   _____

③ Five hundred one and sixty-one hundredths =   _____

④ Forty-eight and two hundred ninety-seven thousandths =   _____

⑤ Fifty and eight hundred twenty-four thousandths =   _____

⑥ Twenty-seven and four hundred nineteen thousandths =   _____

⑦ Ninety-seven and two hundred thirty-five thousandths =   _____

⑧ zero and forty-nine hundredths =   _____

⑨ Twenty-seven and three hundred eighty-five thousandths =   _____

⑩ Seventy-three and eight hundred four thousandths =   _____

⑪ Three hundred eighty-six and twenty hundredths =   _____

⑫ Eight hundred twenty-four and fifty hundredths =   _____

⑬ Four hundred sixty-nine and eighty-one hundredths =   _____

⑭ Six hundred fourteen and fifty-two hundredths =   _____

⑮ Three hundred forty-six and twenty-eight hundredths =   _____

© Libro Studio LLC 2020

Name: _____

Score:

Problems 1-12: *Write the value of each number in written form.*

① 174.38 = _One hundred seventy-four and thirty-eight hundredths_

② 573.49 = _____

③ 908.77 = _____

④ 54.126 = _____

⑤ 61.305 = _____

⑥ 0.420 = _____

⑦ 672.43 = _____

⑧ 734.62 = _____

⑨ 269.83 = _____

⑩ 84.291 = _____

⑪ 31.864 = _____

⑫ 420.17 = _____

© Libro Studio LLC 2020

Name: _____

Score:

Problems 1-15: *Round each number to the nearest:*

		Whole Number	Tenth	Hundredth
①	19.517	20	19.5	19.52
②	104.872			
③	7.067			
④	97.39			
⑤	0.851			
⑥	28.046			
⑦	81.583			
⑧	3.991			
⑨	703.264			
⑩	8.649			
⑪	176.412			
⑫	430.127			
⑬	9.783			
⑭	0.165			
⑮	50.038			

© Libro Studio LLC 2020

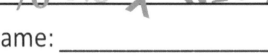

Name: _____

Score:

Problems 1-16: *Round each number to the nearest <u>whole number</u>.*

① 4.501 ② 13.36 ③ 9.72 ④ 0.48

⑤ 1.26 ⑥ 934.61 ⑦ 23.79 ⑧ 5.16

⑨ 7.013 ⑩ 380.84 ⑪ 89.245 ⑫ 419.72

⑬ 59.603 ⑭ 0.489 ⑮ 341.29 ⑯ 48.81

Take a Break
Check Your Work

Problems 17-32: *Round each number to the nearest <u>tenth</u>.*

⑰ 738.13 ⑱ 8.24 ⑲ 439.76 ⑳ 97.68

㉑ 12.371 ㉒ 8.32 ㉓ 74.95 ㉔ 6.86

㉕ 5.77 ㉖ 705.26 ㉗ 0.11 ㉘ 5.83

㉙ 2.39 ㉚ 3.602 ㉛ 69.48 ㉜ 12.345

© Libro Studio LLC 2020

Name: _____

Score:

Problems 1-15: *Round each number to the nearest:*

		Whole Number	Tenth	Hundredth
①	1.385	_____	_____	_____
②	87.614	_____	_____	_____
③	301.572	_____	_____	_____
④	815.04	_____	_____	_____
⑤	6.49	_____	_____	_____
⑥	734.890	_____	_____	_____
⑦	0.76	_____	_____	_____
⑧	281.345	_____	_____	_____
⑨	1.57	_____	_____	_____
⑩	428.91	_____	_____	_____
⑪	9.478	_____	_____	_____
⑫	0.23	_____	_____	_____
⑬	4.671	_____	_____	_____
⑭	601.034	_____	_____	_____
⑮	5.703	_____	_____	_____

© Libro Studio LLC 2020

Problems 1-16: *Round each number to the nearest <u>whole number</u>.*

① 4.501   ② 13.36   ③ 9.72   ④ 0.48

⑤ 35.097   ⑥ 81.64   ⑦ 7.21   ⑧ 5.719

⑨ 612.82   ⑩ 967.30   ⑪ 0.054   ⑫ 97.256

⑬ 0.63   ⑭ 24.96   ⑮ 7.35   ⑯ 4.85

Take a Break
Check Your Work

Problems 17-32: *Round each number to the nearest <u>tenth</u>.*

⑰ 0.28   ⑱ 3.91   ⑲ 209.85   ⑳ 0.127

㉑ 367.69   ㉒ 0.37   ㉓ 978.61   ㉔ 1.639

㉕ 2.265   ㉖ 556.34   ㉗ 6.29   ㉘ 5.324

㉙ 4.714   ㉚ 4.82   ㉛ 618.07   ㉜ 1.66

© Libro Studio LLC 2020

Name: _____

Score:

Problems 1-9: *Round each number to the nearest <u>whole number</u>, then add.*

① 5.62 + 16.554

② 307.93 + 82.1

③ 0.74 + 8.06

④ 0.251 + 524.64

⑤ 7.815 + 6.16

⑥ 111.33 + 26.978

⑦ 82.476 + 9.57

⑧ 801.63 + 0.77

⑨ 3.05 + 4.229

Problems 10-18: *Round each number to the nearest <u>tenth</u>, then add.*

⑩ 266.65 + 6.714

⑪ 9.99 + 728.91

⑫ 0.923 + 88.426

⑬ 570.69 + 172.45

⑭ 1.402 + 5.88

⑮ 2.36 + 421.67

⑯ 3.784 + 4.921

⑰ 3.77 + 9.51

⑱ 0.09 + 6.28

© Libro Studio LLC 2020

Problems 1-9: *Round each number to the nearest <u>whole number</u>, then subtract.*

① **22.82 – 9.63**　　② **5.08 – 0.57**　　③ **310.8 – 14.91**

④ **6.219 – 0.185**　　⑤ **501.34 – 180.43**　　⑥ **861.92 – 428.65**

⑦ **9.01 – 5.15**　　⑧ **7.426 – 2.80**　　⑨ **6.79 – 3.597**

Problems 10-18: *Round each number to the nearest <u>tenth</u>, then subtract.*

⑩ **7.333 – 3.24**　　⑪ **9.69 – 4.302**　　⑫ **0.914 – 0.564**

⑬ **856.71 – 570.17**　　⑭ **21.943 – 9.86**　　⑮ **27.758 – 6.29**

⑯ **801.47 – 171.02**　　⑰ **7.414 – 4.766**　　⑱ **149.83 – 3.88**

© Libro Studio LLC 2020

Day 54
Decimals

Name: _____

Score:

Problems 1-12: *Round each number to the nearest <u>whole number</u>, then add.*

① 27.891 + 5.26 + 2.53

② 0.45 + 6.63 + 4.059

③ 8.22 + 3.718 + 781.92

④ 163.51 + 516.37 + 4.792

⑤ 0.320 + 6.281 + 753.21

⑥ 2.84 + 5.775 + 9.78

⑦ 3.81 + 162.19 + 6.880

⑧ 0.815 + 416.93 + 823.56

⑨ 243.91 + 1.605 + 7.394

⑩ 3.810 + 9.631 + 5.73

⑪ 0.23 + 6.272 + 2.75

⑫ 8.40 + 434.66 + 9.714

© Libro Studio LLC 2020

Name: _____

Score:

Problems 1-15: *Write the number of millions as a decimal:*

		Standard Form	Written Form
①	3,700,000	*3.7 million*	*Three point seven million*
②	48,600,000	_____	_____
③	6,300,000	_____	_____
④	5,100,000	_____	_____
⑤	27,300,000	_____	_____
⑥	9,300,000	_____	_____
⑦	82,500,000	_____	_____
⑧	46,700,000	_____	_____
⑨	3,200,000	_____	_____
⑩	60,400,000	_____	_____
⑪	93,600,000	_____	_____
⑫	7,100,000	_____	_____
⑬	9,900,000	_____	_____
⑭	1,800,000	_____	_____
⑮	76,600,000	_____	_____

© Libro Studio LLC 2020

Name: _____

Score: _____

Problems 1-15: *Write the value of each written number as a standard form decimal.*

Standard Form Decimal:

① Two hundred thirty-eight point six million =   *238.6 million*

② Fifty point one million =   _____

③ Three point five million =   _____

④ One hundred thirty-nine point two million =   _____

⑤ Six point one million =   _____

⑥ Nine point seven million =   _____

⑦ Forty-three point nine million =   _____

⑧ Thirteen point eight million =   _____

⑨ Seventy-eight point five million =   _____

⑩ Two point three million =   _____

⑪ Two hundred fifty-seven point six million =   _____

⑫ Eighty-seven point six million =   _____

⑬ Three point two million =   _____

⑭ Five hundred seven point four million =   _____

⑮ Eight hundred sixty-four point seven million =   _____

© Libro Studio LLC 2020

Name: _____

Score: ___

Problems 1-15: *Write the number of millions as a decimal:*

		Millions as a decimal	**Rounded to the nearest tenth**
①	9,073,857	*9.073857 Million*	*9.1 Million*
②	1,789,204	_____	_____
③	3,958,612	_____	_____
④	7,402,693	_____	_____
⑤	3,015,678	_____	_____
⑥	6,392,851	_____	_____
⑦	9,250,136	_____	_____
⑧	6,843,751	_____	_____
⑨	4,931,025	_____	_____
⑩	8,174,639	_____	_____
⑪	2,369,780	_____	_____
⑫	5,382,019	_____	_____
⑬	7,924,308	_____	_____
⑭	4,019,827	_____	_____
⑮	5,704,180	_____	_____

© Libro Studio LLC 2020

Name: _____

Score: ◯

Problems 1-15: *Write the number of millions as a decimal:*

		Nearest Tenth of a Million	Written Form
①	17,832,105	*17.8 million*	*Seventeen point eight million*
②	7,942,746	_____	_____
③	8,630,519	_____	_____
④	27,960,458	_____	_____
⑤	52,704,107	_____	_____
⑥	85,297,310	_____	_____
⑦	97,362,146	_____	_____
⑧	6,538,124	_____	_____
⑨	31,284,570	_____	_____
⑩	90,742,832	_____	_____
⑪	1,806,543	_____	_____
⑫	4,392,681	_____	_____
⑬	79,032,519	_____	_____
⑭	10,648,253	_____	_____
⑮	2,218,724	_____	_____

© Libro Studio LLC 2020

Name: _____

Score:

Problems 1-16: *Round each number to the nearest <u>tenth of a million</u>.*

① 17,786,021 ② 4,167,029 ③ 1,635,241 ④ 57,521,698

⑤ 2,765,432 ⑥ 18,412,086 ⑦ 3,298,431 ⑧ 4,039,186

⑨ 45,148,269 ⑩ 6,082,175 ⑪ 6,374,707 ⑫ 92,245,640

⑬ 8,301,257 ⑭ 3,652,143 ⑮ 79,864,354 ⑯ 5,996,813

Take a Break
Check Your Work

Problems 17-32: *Round each number to the nearest <u>tenth of a million</u>.*

⑰ 2,089,164 ⑱ 5,864,315 ⑲ 28,293,064 ⑳ 30,613,428

㉑ 7,524,386 ㉒ 44,362,851 ㉓ 1,976,540 ㉔ 51,831,502

㉕ 81,243,765 ㉖ 4,456,210 ㉗ 9,164,832 ㉘ 3,782,193

㉙ 6,100,256 ㉚ 30,972,564 ㉛ 9,726,803 ㉜ 26,499,357

© Libro Studio LLC 2020

Name: _____

Score:

Problems 1-15: *Write the number of millions as a decimal:*

		Millions as a decimal	Rounded to the nearest tenth
①	**873,857**	*0.873857 Million*	*0.9 Million*
②	**6,201,867**	_____	_____
③	**9,724,589**	_____	_____
④	**920,657**	_____	_____
⑤	**36,821,073**	_____	_____
⑥	**9,023,486**	_____	_____
⑦	**7,453,492**	_____	_____
⑧	**11,980,436**	_____	_____
⑨	**4,365,497**	_____	_____
⑩	**87,138,546**	_____	_____
⑪	**1,624,794**	_____	_____
⑫	**8,634,281**	_____	_____
⑬	**12,532,408**	_____	_____
⑭	**58,428,391**	_____	_____
⑮	**792,419**	_____	_____

© Libro Studio LLC 2020

Name: _____

Score:

Problems 1-14: *Round each number to the nearest <u>tenth of a million</u>, then add.*

① **1,623,457 + 9,581,230**

② **8,278,691 + 7,382,469**

③ **6,200,206 + 5,553,364**

④ **34,032,416 + 18,832,949**

⑤ **9,570,133 + 1,816,231**

⑥ **2,713,450 + 33,621,493**

⑦ **51,215,739 + 26,712,390**

⑧ **7,113,949 + 8,702,856**

⑨ **1,324,988 + 2,072,463**

⑩ **32,678,421 + 14,821,934**

⑪ **59,278,938 + 8,867,242**

⑫ **7,302,487 + 6,198,234**

⑬ **25,023,946 + 54,765,431**

⑭ **13,516,789 + 62,900,245**

© Libro Studio LLC 2020

Name: _____

Score:

Problems 1-14: *Round each number to the nearest <u>tenth of a million</u>, then add.*

① 58,134,560 + 4,545,698

② 29,468,123 + 65,076,328

③ 3,826,105 + 7,015,786

④ 51,279,123 + 16,986,317

⑤ 2,426,907 + 6,330,245

⑥ 11,116,381 + 5,368,159

⑦ 42,831,624 + 6,491,267

⑧ 31,246,893 + 9,615,490

⑨ 7,253,476 + 73,102,794

⑩ 18,219,062 + 14,526,318

⑪ 18,670,254 + 34,792,131

⑫ 49,762,180 + 5,683,219

⑬ 3,712,760 + 7,572,304

⑭ 2,198,735 + 2,325,641

© Libro Studio LLC 2020

Name: _____

Score:

Problems 1-12: *Round each number to the nearest* <u>*tenth of a million*</u>, *then add.*

①
6,487,125
11,210,235
+ 5,162,154

②
19,721,851
54,862,130
+ 8,584,069

③
21,823,767
6,251,384
+ 2,432,610

④
3,931,624
37,512,346
+ 22,792,110

⑤
7,076,665
3,702,613
+ 18,246,891

⑥
4,167,290
9,626,881
+ 5,402,056

⑦
4,997,762
8,722,113
+ 3,241,687

⑧
17,612,397
12,362,452
+ 6,198,031

⑨
13,384,444
57,506,218
+ 12,076,249

⑩
1,726,389
5,982,637
+ 9,612,541

⑪
6,209,872
1,475,316
+ 5,552,173

⑫
19,989,870
4,621,916
+ 28,301,038

© Libro Studio LLC 2020

Name: _____

Score:

Problems 1-12: *Round each number to the nearest <u>tenth of a million</u>, then add.*

①
4,435,466
8,012,365
+ 3,663,378

②
7,902,450
42,429,765
+ 6,392,639

③
13,816,717
17,750,264
+ 21,897,000

④
11,246,324
35,400,228
+ 9,789,673

⑤
6,200,236
1,723,674
+ 5,630,298

⑥
59,019,763
4,881,367
+ 8,630,202

⑦
41,233,008
15,372,189
+ 19,306,241

⑧
4,240,069
8,063,142
+ 3,127,936

⑨
7,861,231
2,793,255
+ 6,621,939

⑩
12,972,613
6,563,124
+ 11,080,137

⑪
28,378,332
33,542,196
+ 27,210,201

⑫
15,113,057
9,559,623
+ 4,402,377

© Libro Studio LLC 2020

Name: _____

Score:

Problems 1-5: *Shade the shapes to represents each fraction. (You may not need to use all the shapes shown).*

① $4\frac{1}{2}$

② $6\frac{2}{3}$

③ $2\frac{5}{6}$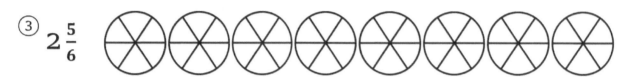

④ $\frac{1}{4}$

⑤ $3\frac{1}{3}$

Problems 6-10: *Write a fraction to represent the amount of shaded shapes.*

⑥ ____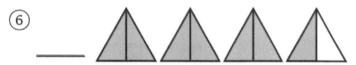

⑦ ____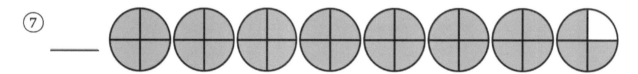

⑧ ____

⑨ ____

⑩ ____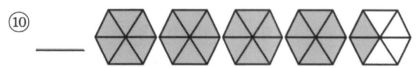

© Libro Studio LLC 2020

Name: _____

Score:

Problems 1-10: *Write the value of each written fraction in standard form.*

Standard Form:

$13\frac{1}{3}$

① thirteen and one-third = _____

② Six and four-ninths = _____

③ One and five-sixths = _____

④ Seven and two-thirds = _____

⑤ Thirty-four and one half = _____

⑥ Four and seven over twenty = _____

⑦ Twelve and three-fifths = _____

⑧ Ten and thirteen over sixteen = _____

⑨ Three-fourths = _____

⑩ Eight and eight over twenty-five = _____

Problems 11-15: *Write the value of each fraction in written form.*

⑪ $5\frac{3}{7}$ = *Five and three-sevenths*

⑫ $2\frac{2}{5}$ = _____

⑬ $1\frac{9}{10}$ = _____

⑭ $\frac{4}{9}$ = _____

⑮ $4\frac{1}{2}$ = _____

© Libro Studio LLC 2020

Name: _____

Score:

Rounding Fractions

Round Down: If the fraction is less than one half, round down.
Round Up: If the fraction is greater than or equal to one half, round up.

Hint: *It helps to make the denominators the same.*
Examples:

$\frac{3}{10}$	$\frac{2}{3}$	$\frac{1}{7}$	$\frac{2}{4}$
$\frac{3}{10} < \frac{1}{2}$	$\frac{2}{3} > \frac{1}{2}$	$\frac{1}{7} < \frac{1}{2}$	$\frac{2}{4} = \frac{1}{2}$
$\frac{3}{10} < \frac{5}{10}$	$\frac{2}{3} > \frac{1.5}{3}$	$\frac{1}{7} < \frac{3.5}{7}$	$\frac{2}{4} = \frac{2}{4}$
Round Down	**Round Up**	**Round Down**	**Round Up**

Problems 1-8: *Round each fraction to the nearest whole number. Circle the correct answer.*

(Less than half)   (Greater than or equal to half)
Round Down   *or*   **Round Up**

① 3 ← $3\frac{3}{10}$ → 4

② 9 ← $9\frac{1}{4}$ → 10

③ 20 ← $20\frac{4}{5}$ → 21

④ 0 ← $\frac{3}{6}$ → 1

⑤ 2 ← $2\frac{7}{8}$ → 3

⑥ 15 ← $15\frac{5}{12}$ → 16

⑦ 8 ← $8\frac{4}{9}$ → 9

⑧ 6 ← $6\frac{1}{3}$ → 7

© Libro Studio LLC 2020

Day 68
Rounding Fractions

Name: _____

Score:

Problems 1-15: *Fill in the blanks, then round each fraction to the nearest whole number.*

(Less than half)		(Greater than or equal to half)
Round Down	*or*	**Round Up**

① _____ ⬅ $1\frac{5}{13}$ ➡ _____

② _____ ⬅ $16\frac{5}{10}$ ➡ _____

③ _____ ⬅ $\frac{3}{7}$ ➡ _____

④ _____ ⬅ $9\frac{5}{8}$ ➡ _____

⑤ _____ ⬅ $3\frac{2}{5}$ ➡ _____

⑥ _____ ⬅ $12\frac{2}{3}$ ➡ _____

⑦ _____ ⬅ $\frac{11}{20}$ ➡ _____

⑧ _____ ⬅ $5\frac{7}{14}$ ➡ _____

⑨ _____ ⬅ $2\frac{37}{100}$ ➡ _____

⑩ _____ ⬅ $3\frac{7}{11}$ ➡ _____

⑪ _____ ⬅ $4\frac{9}{12}$ ➡ _____

⑫ _____ ⬅ $27\frac{3}{5}$ ➡ _____

⑬ _____ ⬅ $14\frac{1}{4}$ ➡ _____

⑭ _____ ⬅ $3\frac{4}{8}$ ➡ _____

⑮ _____ ⬅ $\frac{6}{12}$ ➡ _____

© Libro Studio LLC 2020

Name: _____

Score:

Problems 1-15: *Fill in the blanks, then round each fraction to the nearest whole number.*

(Less than half)		(Greater than or equal to half)
Round Down	*or*	**Round Up**

① _____ ← $7\frac{5}{6}$ → _____

② _____ ← $2\frac{3}{13}$ → _____

③ _____ ← $8\frac{7}{9}$ → _____

④ _____ ← $1\frac{4}{10}$ → _____

⑤ _____ ← $\frac{6}{10}$ → _____

⑥ _____ ← $\frac{7}{14}$ → _____

⑦ _____ ← $23\frac{6}{13}$ → _____

⑧ _____ ← $3\frac{8}{9}$ → _____

⑨ _____ ← $4\frac{1}{5}$ → _____

⑩ _____ ← $9\frac{6}{8}$ → _____

⑪ _____ ← $\frac{3}{7}$ → _____

⑫ _____ ← $45\frac{20}{30}$ → _____

⑬ _____ ← $5\frac{4}{8}$ → _____

⑭ _____ ← $13\frac{8}{20}$ → _____

⑮ _____ ← $6\frac{10}{16}$ → _____

© Libro Studio LLC 2020

Name: _____

Score:

Problems 1-20: *Round each fraction to the nearest whole number.*

① $5\frac{2}{6}$ ② $8\frac{7}{15}$ ③ $11\frac{8}{9}$ ④ $\frac{4}{10}$ ⑤ $19\frac{9}{18}$

⑥ $50\frac{33}{34}$ ⑦ $1\frac{5}{9}$ ⑧ $8\frac{11}{18}$ ⑨ $25\frac{1}{2}$ ⑩ $7\frac{8}{18}$

⑪ $15\frac{12}{20}$ ⑫ $\frac{4}{7}$ ⑬ $\frac{40}{100}$ ⑭ $3\frac{3}{30}$ ⑮ $4\frac{4}{5}$

⑯ $33\frac{7}{9}$ ⑰ $2\frac{3}{8}$ ⑱ $1\frac{7}{15}$ ⑲ $6\frac{2}{5}$ ⑳ $3\frac{10}{16}$

Take a Break
Check Your Work

Problems 21-40: *Round each fraction to the nearest whole number.*

㉑ $\frac{7}{12}$ ㉒ $1\frac{3}{6}$ ㉓ $7\frac{2}{8}$ ㉔ $11\frac{1}{2}$ ㉕ $3\frac{5}{10}$

㉖ $8\frac{2}{5}$ ㉗ $5\frac{1}{3}$ ㉘ $33\frac{3}{6}$ ㉙ $2\frac{6}{11}$ ㉚ $\frac{80}{100}$

㉛ $9\frac{7}{9}$ ㉜ $4\frac{7}{16}$ ㉝ $6\frac{8}{13}$ ㉞ $\frac{5}{6}$ ㉟ $5\frac{5}{9}$

㊱ $14\frac{13}{20}$ ㊲ $13\frac{3}{11}$ ㊳ $21\frac{24}{25}$ ㊴ $25\frac{9}{18}$ ㊵ $10\frac{12}{16}$

© Libro Studio LLC 2020

Name: _____

Score:

Problems 1-20: *Round each fraction to the nearest whole number.*

① $1\frac{4}{9}$ ② $3\frac{2}{7}$ ③ $34\frac{3}{5}$ ④ $\frac{6}{7}$ ⑤ $5\frac{1}{6}$

⑥ $20\frac{5}{10}$ ⑦ $\frac{9}{20}$ ⑧ $11\frac{5}{6}$ ⑨ $10\frac{2}{10}$ ⑩ $4\frac{11}{12}$

⑪ $2\frac{11}{15}$ ⑫ $6\frac{3}{4}$ ⑬ $9\frac{4}{5}$ ⑭ $7\frac{25}{50}$ ⑮ $\frac{5}{11}$

⑯ $54\frac{2}{6}$ ⑰ $16\frac{2}{3}$ ⑱ $\frac{30}{50}$ ⑲ $15\frac{17}{20}$ ⑳ $13\frac{7}{13}$

Take a Break
Check Your Work

Problems 21-40: *Round each fraction to the nearest whole number.*

㉑ $4\frac{1}{5}$ ㉒ $9\frac{5}{8}$ ㉓ $\frac{3}{10}$ ㉔ $2\frac{20}{25}$ ㉕ $6\frac{5}{9}$

㉖ $8\frac{13}{20}$ ㉗ $\frac{17}{100}$ ㉘ $1\frac{10}{19}$ ㉙ $7\frac{2}{3}$ ㉚ $3\frac{1}{4}$

㉛ $5\frac{1}{2}$ ㉜ $43\frac{5}{7}$ ㉝ $80\frac{3}{9}$ ㉞ $11\frac{6}{7}$ ㉟ $15\frac{7}{20}$

㊱ $\frac{9}{18}$ ㊲ $12\frac{2}{4}$ ㊳ $32\frac{4}{6}$ ㊴ $\frac{22}{50}$ ㊵ $26\frac{11}{16}$

© Libro Studio LLC 2020

Name: _____

Score:

Problems 1-20: *Round each fraction to the nearest whole number.*

① $12\frac{1}{2}$ ② $2\frac{36}{50}$ ③ $9\frac{11}{20}$ ④ $3\frac{7}{16}$ ⑤ $15\frac{8}{19}$

⑥ $5\frac{5}{25}$ ⑦ $4\frac{8}{13}$ ⑧ $\frac{15}{32}$ ⑨ $\frac{8}{17}$ ⑩ $5\frac{11}{22}$

⑪ $11\frac{6}{20}$ ⑫ $22\frac{6}{9}$ ⑬ $27\frac{3}{6}$ ⑭ $7\frac{9}{14}$ ⑮ $1\frac{10}{30}$

⑯ $13\frac{2}{3}$ ⑰ $39\frac{6}{7}$ ⑱ $80\frac{2}{5}$ ⑲ $1\frac{1}{4}$ ⑳ $6\frac{6}{12}$

Take a Break
Check Your Work

Problems 21-40: *Round each fraction to the nearest whole number.*

㉑ $5\frac{8}{14}$ ㉒ $11\frac{2}{100}$ ㉓ $7\frac{7}{15}$ ㉔ $4\frac{13}{30}$ ㉕ $9\frac{7}{18}$

㉖ $75\frac{3}{5}$ ㉗ $\frac{87}{100}$ ㉘ $13\frac{10}{23}$ ㉙ $\frac{5}{11}$ ㉚ $8\frac{4}{9}$

㉛ $2\frac{9}{18}$ ㉜ $1\frac{7}{11}$ ㉝ $15\frac{3}{15}$ ㉞ $\frac{6}{8}$ ㉟ $3\frac{5}{20}$

㊱ $11\frac{7}{12}$ ㊲ $50\frac{5}{10}$ ㊳ $84\frac{15}{40}$ ㊴ $51\frac{6}{13}$ ㊵ $6\frac{8}{15}$

© Libro Studio LLC 2020

Name: _____

Score:

Problems 1-20: *Round each fraction to the nearest whole number.*

① $4\frac{2}{5}$ ② $6\frac{13}{16}$ ③ $7\frac{5}{11}$ ④ $1\frac{19}{50}$ ⑤ $2\frac{30}{60}$

⑥ $\frac{9}{20}$ ⑦ $5\frac{25}{80}$ ⑧ $99\frac{9}{12}$ ⑨ $3\frac{14}{20}$ ⑩ $\frac{8}{17}$

⑪ $8\frac{3}{7}$ ⑫ $24\frac{9}{16}$ ⑬ $15\frac{1}{5}$ ⑭ $30\frac{5}{9}$ ⑮ $91\frac{5}{8}$

⑯ $53\frac{3}{9}$ ⑰ $10\frac{38}{80}$ ⑱ $5\frac{30}{40}$ ⑲ $2\frac{11}{16}$ ⑳ $\frac{61}{100}$

Take a Break
Check Your Work

Problems 21-40: *Round each fraction to the nearest whole number.*

㉑ $8\frac{10}{15}$ ㉒ $15\frac{3}{8}$ ㉓ $1\frac{25}{100}$ ㉔ $\frac{27}{80}$ ㉕ $\frac{25}{40}$

㉖ $10\frac{8}{18}$ ㉗ $9\frac{3}{33}$ ㉘ $22\frac{1}{2}$ ㉙ $16\frac{11}{12}$ ㉚ $35\frac{5}{6}$

㉛ $\frac{35}{40}$ ㉜ $\frac{15}{50}$ ㉝ $6\frac{3}{24}$ ㉞ $7\frac{9}{16}$ ㉟ $1\frac{8}{32}$

㊱ $3\frac{9}{55}$ ㊲ $24\frac{4}{24}$ ㊳ $62\frac{6}{12}$ ㊴ $59\frac{5}{9}$ ㊵ $2\frac{7}{30}$

© Libro Studio LLC 2020

Name: _____

Score:

Problems 1-20: *Round each fraction to the nearest whole number.*

① $11 \frac{6}{16}$ ② $\frac{3}{17}$ ③ $5 \frac{1}{20}$ ④ $9 \frac{2}{3}$ ⑤ $6 \frac{8}{80}$

⑥ $8 \frac{7}{17}$ ⑦ $4 \frac{6}{14}$ ⑧ $\frac{27}{50}$ ⑨ $3 \frac{6}{10}$ ⑩ $\frac{5}{100}$

⑪ $7 \frac{21}{22}$ ⑫ $10 \frac{9}{11}$ ⑬ $\frac{4}{20}$ ⑭ $27 \frac{1}{2}$ ⑮ $16 \frac{5}{14}$

⑯ $13 \frac{18}{22}$ ⑰ $29 \frac{2}{3}$ ⑱ $12 \frac{6}{7}$ ⑲ $20 \frac{3}{4}$ ⑳ $17 \frac{8}{14}$

Take a Break
Check Your Work

Problems 21-40: *Round each fraction to the nearest whole number.*

㉑ $9 \frac{6}{25}$ ㉒ $1 \frac{14}{30}$ ㉓ $5 \frac{7}{24}$ ㉔ $2 \frac{2}{9}$ ㉕ $17 \frac{1}{2}$

㉖ $10 \frac{1}{4}$ ㉗ $3 \frac{3}{7}$ ㉘ $\frac{10}{22}$ ㉙ $\frac{11}{18}$ ㉚ $7 \frac{2}{5}$

㉛ $\frac{50}{60}$ ㉜ $41 \frac{3}{9}$ ㉝ $16 \frac{2}{6}$ ㉞ $8 \frac{10}{17}$ ㉟ $4 \frac{35}{80}$

㊱ $18 \frac{3}{14}$ ㊲ $6 \frac{2}{5}$ ㊳ $49 \frac{1}{2}$ ㊴ $11 \frac{1}{9}$ ㊵ $\frac{30}{50}$

© Libro Studio LLC 2020

Name: _____

Score:

Problems 1-20: *Round each fraction to the nearest whole number.*

① $2\frac{3}{19}$

② $9\frac{1}{6}$

③ $5\frac{4}{12}$

④ $1\frac{7}{12}$

⑤ $24\frac{9}{11}$

⑥ $19\frac{3}{6}$

⑦ $91\frac{1}{2}$

⑧ $\frac{2}{8}$

⑨ $\frac{12}{100}$

⑩ $8\frac{13}{14}$

⑪ $6\frac{13}{20}$

⑫ $3\frac{10}{50}$

⑬ $4\frac{8}{22}$

⑭ $7\frac{10}{100}$

⑮ $10\frac{6}{13}$

⑯ $\frac{15}{35}$

⑰ $\frac{20}{50}$

⑱ $11\frac{11}{12}$

⑲ $13\frac{7}{17}$

⑳ $12\frac{20}{25}$

Take a Break
Check Your Work

Problems 21-40: *Round each fraction to the nearest whole number.*

㉑ $8\frac{2}{8}$

㉒ $1\frac{8}{13}$

㉓ $5\frac{5}{40}$

㉔ $7\frac{9}{20}$

㉕ $10\frac{4}{20}$

㉖ $2\frac{3}{7}$

㉗ $4\frac{14}{28}$

㉘ $9\frac{7}{21}$

㉙ $6\frac{2}{16}$

㉚ $3\frac{3}{9}$

㉛ $16\frac{3}{6}$

㉜ $21\frac{1}{2}$

㉝ $30\frac{6}{9}$

㉞ $2\frac{8}{9}$

㉟ $5\frac{11}{17}$

㊱ $7\frac{5}{24}$

㊲ $9\frac{2}{9}$

㊳ $27\frac{1}{5}$

㊴ $\frac{16}{30}$

㊵ $\frac{71}{80}$

© Libro Studio LLC 2020

Name: _____

Score: _____

Problems 1-24: *Round each fraction to the nearest whole number, then add.*

① $5\frac{2}{4} + 7\frac{2}{5} =$

② $9\frac{5}{7} + 6\frac{1}{2} =$

③ $2\frac{3}{8} + 13\frac{1}{3} =$

④ $3\frac{7}{14} + 8\frac{1}{4} =$

⑤ $4\frac{3}{9} + 11\frac{6}{12} =$

⑥ $2\frac{9}{17} + 1\frac{10}{18} =$

⑦ $14\frac{3}{5} + 10\frac{7}{10} =$

⑧ $2\frac{4}{6} + 1\frac{11}{20} =$

⑨ $8\frac{4}{30} + 18\frac{2}{5} =$

⑩ $6\frac{18}{24} + 9\frac{15}{50} =$

⑪ $15\frac{7}{25} + 3\frac{33}{40} =$

⑫ $1\frac{14}{15} + 7\frac{3}{28} =$

⑬ $17\frac{1}{12} + 31\frac{8}{17} =$

⑭ $7\frac{6}{11} + 2\frac{19}{100} =$

⑮ $12\frac{14}{22} + 3\frac{8}{18} =$

⑯ $7\frac{9}{11} + 5\frac{6}{11} =$

⑰ $13\frac{1}{71} + 12\frac{1}{72} =$

⑱ $9\frac{6}{7} + 3\frac{1}{3} =$

⑲ $1\frac{15}{35} + 2\frac{1}{15} =$

⑳ $4\frac{20}{28} + 8\frac{40}{50} =$

㉑ $7\frac{7}{24} + 5\frac{10}{15} =$

㉒ $7\frac{1}{2} + 6\frac{2}{3} =$

㉓ $9\frac{9}{20} + 3\frac{3}{7} =$

㉔ $6\frac{3}{5} + 10\frac{2}{8} =$

© Libro Studio LLC 2020

Name: _____

Score:

Problems 1-24: *Round each fraction to the nearest whole number, then add.*

① $1\frac{2}{7} + 3\frac{5}{25} =$

② $7\frac{3}{10} + 4\frac{6}{12} =$

③ $10\frac{7}{14} + 5\frac{6}{15} =$

④ $2\frac{6}{9} + 6\frac{3}{18} =$

⑤ $9\frac{11}{50} + 11\frac{21}{30} =$

⑥ $17\frac{1}{2} + 5\frac{12}{17} =$

⑦ $8\frac{3}{12} + 5\frac{9}{30} =$

⑧ $12\frac{2}{5} + 9\frac{5}{9} =$

⑨ $4\frac{6}{12} + 1\frac{10}{16} =$

⑩ $9\frac{2}{5} + 1\frac{8}{14} =$

⑪ $16\frac{1}{4} + 15\frac{3}{4} =$

⑫ $27\frac{9}{15} + 3\frac{8}{14} =$

⑬ $6\frac{6}{10} + 13\frac{6}{17} =$

⑭ $9\frac{4}{8} + 7\frac{5}{16} =$

⑮ $2\frac{18}{30} + 5\frac{7}{18} =$

⑯ $11\frac{1}{3} + 5\frac{2}{7} =$

⑰ $6\frac{15}{16} + 1\frac{20}{40} =$

⑱ $20\frac{3}{8} + 11\frac{3}{7} =$

⑲ $7\frac{60}{100} + 1\frac{6}{8} =$

⑳ $13\frac{3}{4} + 2\frac{6}{7} =$

㉑ $13\frac{8}{16} + 4\frac{4}{10} =$

㉒ $10\frac{3}{6} + 10\frac{7}{20} =$

㉓ $3\frac{6}{13} + 2\frac{8}{15} =$

㉔ $5\frac{11}{22} + 6\frac{4}{9} =$

© Libro Studio LLC 2020

Name: _____

Problems 1-24: *Round each fraction to the nearest whole number, then subtract.*

① $5\frac{3}{13} - 1\frac{1}{6} =$

② $20\frac{4}{5} - 10\frac{6}{9} =$

③ $9\frac{2}{4} - 6\frac{3}{12} =$

④ $12\frac{12}{24} - 2\frac{4}{10} =$

⑤ $8\frac{1}{2} - 3\frac{2}{6} =$

⑥ $17\frac{5}{10} - 7\frac{7}{20} =$

⑦ $8\frac{20}{60} - 5\frac{5}{8} =$

⑧ $21\frac{4}{7} - 15\frac{2}{10} =$

⑨ $6\frac{7}{16} - 4\frac{15}{32} =$

⑩ $11\frac{2}{3} - 4\frac{3}{11} =$

⑪ $13\frac{10}{24} - 6\frac{5}{14} =$

⑫ $18\frac{7}{12} - 8\frac{1}{3} =$

⑬ $5\frac{7}{18} - 3\frac{6}{11} =$

⑭ $7\frac{13}{20} - 4\frac{7}{15} =$

⑮ $14\frac{2}{4} - 6\frac{9}{14} =$

⑯ $12\frac{2}{11} - 10\frac{8}{9} =$

⑰ $6\frac{4}{15} - 2\frac{4}{8} =$

⑱ $3\frac{7}{19} - 1\frac{3}{13} =$

⑲ $5\frac{30}{40} - 1\frac{8}{20} =$

⑳ $9\frac{6}{13} - 4\frac{11}{25} =$

㉑ $11\frac{5}{15} - 2\frac{7}{18} =$

㉒ $8\frac{4}{7} - 7\frac{4}{9} =$

㉓ $7\frac{7}{11} - 6\frac{1}{7} =$

㉔ $3\frac{10}{30} - 1\frac{11}{19} =$

© Libro Studio LLC 2020

Name: _____

Score:

Problems 1-24: *Round each fraction to the nearest whole number, then subtract.*

① $2 \frac{3}{21} - 1 \frac{1}{2} =$

② $11 \frac{6}{9} - 5 \frac{7}{12} =$

③ $7 \frac{3}{8} - 6 \frac{1}{2} =$

④ $3 \frac{9}{18} - 1 \frac{15}{22} =$

⑤ $15 \frac{6}{7} - 12 \frac{4}{5} =$

⑥ $10 \frac{3}{4} - 8 \frac{3}{6} =$

⑦ $21 \frac{1}{2} - 6 \frac{3}{5} =$

⑧ $7 \frac{7}{15} - 5 \frac{6}{7} =$

⑨ $17 \frac{14}{20} - 1 \frac{8}{16} =$

⑩ $8 \frac{9}{11} - 6 \frac{3}{10} =$

⑪ $13 \frac{4}{6} - 8 \frac{1}{6} =$

⑫ $9 \frac{5}{10} - 4 \frac{10}{19} =$

⑬ $5 \frac{3}{9} - 3 \frac{3}{12} =$

⑭ $15 \frac{17}{40} - 12 \frac{6}{15} =$

⑮ $19 \frac{10}{20} - 2 \frac{6}{13} =$

⑯ $11 \frac{8}{30} - 9 \frac{9}{16} =$

⑰ $6 \frac{7}{12} - 5 \frac{3}{4} =$

⑱ $10 \frac{6}{10} - 2 \frac{6}{20} =$

⑲ $13 \frac{11}{13} - 7 \frac{7}{16} =$

⑳ $8 \frac{1}{3} - 4 \frac{2}{4} =$

㉑ $18 \frac{4}{9} - 8 \frac{5}{8} =$

㉒ $6 \frac{12}{16} - 3 \frac{8}{12} =$

㉓ $15 \frac{3}{15} - 4 \frac{6}{14} =$

㉔ $9 \frac{15}{18} - 3 \frac{3}{9} =$

© Libro Studio LLC 2020

Name: _____

Score:

Trillions			Billions			Millions			Thousands			Ones		
Hundred Trillions	Ten Trillions	Trillions	Hundred Billions	Ten Billions	Billions	Hundred Millions	Ten Millions	Millions	Hundred Thousands	Ten Thousands	Thousands	Hundreds	Tens	Ones
3	6	8	9	7	4	1	9	2	6	5	8	3	7	5

Problems 1-15: *Write the value of each underlined digit in number form and written form.*

		Number Form:	**Written Form:**
①	9<u>4</u>5,185,303,076,875	*40,000,000,000,000*	*Forty trillion*
②	709,63<u>4</u>,815,213,501		
③	<u>9</u>58,214,367,086,956		
④	675,<u>2</u>46,890,165,734		
⑤	3<u>6</u>2,479,580,129,083		
⑥	20<u>7</u>,489,651,380,621		
⑦	523,97<u>6</u>,104,856,752		
⑧	841,9<u>5</u>7,083,267,390		
⑨	8<u>1</u>6,245,370,963,846		
⑩	501,<u>2</u>79,436,830,154		
⑪	18<u>9</u>,326,540,790,108		
⑫	417,<u>3</u>90,682,517,639		
⑬	72<u>6</u>,349,501,823,745		
⑭	98<u>7</u>,654,321,012,345		
⑮	625,34<u>1</u>,798,280,142		

© Libro Studio LLC 2020

Name: _____

Score:

Problems 1-15: *Write the value of each written number in standard form.*

Standard Form:

① Thirty-two trillion, six hundred three billion, five hundred eighty-four million, nine hundred sixty-six thousand, one hundred fourteen

32,603,584,966,114

② Eight trillion, six hundred thirty billion, four hundred fifty-eight million, nine hundred twenty-seven thousand, seven hundred fifteen

_____

③ Forty-seven trillion, eighty-five thousand, three hundred ninety-four

_____

④ Seventy-four trillion, five hundred sixty-seven billion, eight hundred ninety million, four hundred thirty-one thousand, two hundred forty-three

_____

⑤ Ten trillion, two hundred eighty-three billion, seven hundred forty-five million, six hundred ninety thousand, nine hundred eighty

_____

⑥ Three trillion, eight hundred thirty-one billion, five hundred sixty-nine million, two hundred thousand

_____

⑦ Twenty trillion, nine hundred thirteen billion, seven hundred fifty-six million, eight hundred twenty-four thousand, seven hundred thirty-two

_____

⑧ Fifty-three trillion, twelve billion, three hundred forty-five million, six hundred seventy-eight thousand, nine hundred eighteen

_____

⑨ Eighty-six trillion, one hundred seven billion, five hundred forty-three million, two hundred eighteen thousand, six hundred one

_____

⑩ Twenty trillion, seven hundred eighty million, two hundred sixty-one thousand

_____

⑪ Six trillion, six hundred eighty billion, nine hundred seventy-two thousand, four hundred eighty-nine

_____

⑫ Thirty-eight trillion, one hundred sixty-seven billion, two hundred forty-five million, nine hundred seven thousand, five hundred sixty-seven

_____

⑬ Sixty-two trillion, seven hundred ninety-one billion, three hundred sixty-eight million, one hundred eighty thousand, three hundred forty-nine

_____

⑭ Nine trillion, seven hundred twenty-six billion, three hundred fifty-four million, eight hundred eight thousand, three hundred forty-six

_____

⑮ Thirty-nine trillion, two hundred fourteen billion, six hundred seventy-five million, eight hundred thirty thousand, five hundred forty-four

_____

© Libro Studio LLC 2020

Name: _____

Score:

Problems 1-9: *Write the value of each number in written form.*

① 134,890,043,629,170 = <u>One hundred thirty-four trillion, eight hundred ninety</u>
   <u>billion, forty-three million, six hundred twenty-nine thousand, one hundred</u>
   <u>seventy</u>

② 445,678,901,284,657 = _____

③ 863,241,000,178,630 = _____

④ 12,760,398,846,743 = _____

⑤ 1,063,518,409,281 = _____

⑥ 956,204,187,621,000 = _____

⑦ 78,754,321,098,268 = _____

⑧ 580,123,678,593,419 = _____

⑨ 20,598,763,471,805 = _____

© Libro Studio LLC 2020

Name: _____

Score:

Problems 1-20: *Round each number to the nearest:*

		Trillion:	Ten Billion:
①	615,764,821,505,930	*616,000,000,000,000*	*615,760,000,000,000*
②	192,836,475,021,934		
③	5,712,864,970,651		
④	538,620,419,791,269		
⑤	79,302,145,897,265		
⑥	93,867,243,570,312		
⑦	270,487,591,856,974		
⑧	429,916,359,012,807		
⑨	3,157,980,342,751		
⑩	860,231,076,980,384		
⑪	19,830,216,748,967		
⑫	216,357,498,641,280		
⑬	479,050,143,267,596		
⑭	7,912,365,407,827		
⑮	826,302,579,167,246		
⑯	17,280,743,990,289		
⑰	354,167,102,781,340		
⑱	1,648,460,509,216		
⑲	709,274,316,725,119		
⑳	90,457,860,024,156		

© Libro Studio LLC 2020

Name: _____

Score:

Problems 1-20: *Write the number of billions as a decimal rounded to the nearest tenth.*

		Nearest Tenth of a Billion	Written Form
①	85,353,076,875	*85.4 billion*	*eighty-five point four billion*
②	94,821,365,957		
③	64,261,389,705		
④	36,912,345,678		
⑤	96,070,412,388		
⑥	62,730,481,665		
⑦	30,514,876,297		
⑧	42,781,360,594		
⑨	78,247,120,890		
⑩	15,953,861,241		
⑪	43,500,862,913		
⑫	70,012,867,199		
⑬	19,289,376,450		
⑭	29,167,840,352		
⑮	57,890,164,727		
⑯	27,819,609,154		
⑰	51,246,875,129		
⑱	89,100,653,427		
⑲	24,738,913,876		
⑳	81,689,375,489		

© Libro Studio LLC 2020

Problems 1-9: *Round each number to the nearest <u>tenth of a billion</u>, then add.*

①   2,577,444,222
  + 36,148,306,139

②   85,263,917,650
  + 49,390,812,456

③   7,019,542,674
  + 2,489,153,946

④   19,786,342,176
  + 4,251,879,300

⑤   95,361,258,666
  + 53,900,160,453

⑥   4,376,908,132
  + 61,255,676,835

⑦   10,134,579,828
  + 3,867,901,425

⑧   8,605,187,343
  +   781,246,505

⑨   47,243,350,169
  + 26,123,462,918

Problems 10-18: *Round each number to the nearest <u>tenth of a trillion</u>, then add.*

⑩   3,249,578,061,458
  +   951,830,745,307

⑪   8,360,712,463,871
  + 6,110,010,169,723

⑫   2,220,020,278,654
  + 9,731,456,809,926

⑬   568,712,394,180
  + 5,490,678,193,272

⑭   14,689,736,286,111
  + 98,268,442,462,059

⑮   4,951,628,730,725
  + 2,413,896,057,081

⑯   62,628,828,484,378
  + 6,304,414,787,501

⑰   7,810,356,293,086
  + 6,073,247,958,437

⑱   3,863,593,141,609
  + 76,696,086,282,135

© Libro Studio LLC 2020

Name: _____

Score:

Problems 1-9: *Round each number to the nearest <u>tenth of a billion</u>, then add.*

①
1,924,307,532
+ 7,284,506,937

②
3,194,229,779
+ 78,475,961,208

③
4,466,886,816
+ 5,831,789,065

④
24,910,723,842
+ 27,531,790,517

⑤
2,282,448,468
+ 36,801,203,460

⑥
95,136,892,304
+ 8,822,662,693

⑦
19,370,513,953
+   602,406,820

⑧
42,288,448,448
+ 76,648,224,285

⑨
83,709,524,196
+ 4,464,886,828

Problems 10-18: *Round each number to the nearest <u>tenth of a trillion</u>, then add.*

⑩
92,501,632,894,245
+ 64,921,356,702,698

⑪
7,602,543,821,656
+ 5,812,456,720,377

⑫
6,294,307,158,963
+ 50,386,457,091,248

⑬
57,361,248,600,299
+ 85,046,391,495,713

⑭
630,159,473,561
+ 21,956,748,309,484

⑮
3,971,245,806,654
+ 49,183,926,570,897

⑯
14,632,798,063,941
+ 1,954,368,023,792

⑰
43,169,345,620,945
+ 8,243,679,015,863

⑱
8,510,289,361,909
+ 9,680,154,736,209

© Libro Studio LLC 2020

Name: _____

Score:

Problems 1-9: *Round each number to the nearest <u>tenth of a billion</u>, then add.*

①   9,862,345,701
   + 56,012,345,678

②   7,654,123,096
   + 5,329,154,672

③   736,451,294
   + 26,578,910,346

④   30,123,456,789
   + 77,345,678,987

⑤   8,086,145,675
   +   875,634,103

⑥   2,987,654,301
   + 13,248,357,698

⑦   28,976,543,210
   + 61,254,873,901

⑧   5,678,901,234
   + 3,456,789,012

⑨   34,702,356,129
   + 75,634,712,817

Problems 10-18: *Round each number to the nearest <u>tenth of a trillion</u>, then add.*

⑩   9,303,124,567,840
   + 3,579,821,036,421

⑪   6,219,346,549,207
   + 94,268,789,631,151

⑫   61,639,578,269,124
   + 38,193,456,240,156

⑬   7,231,895,740,863
   + 22,807,165,349,249

⑭   6,749,312,807,545
   + 9,624,310,879,246

⑮   83,216,313,872,459
   +   896,743,210,876

⑯   4,260,359,786,241
   + 4,912,654,821,360

⑰   76,413,205,874,561
   + 17,689,702,541,302

⑱   72,816,503,952,608
   + 8,017,635,948,255

© Libro Studio LLC 2020

Name: _____

Score: _____

Problems 1-9: *Round each number to the nearest <u>tenth of a billion</u>, then subtract.*

①   2,087,242,867
    − 1,867,244,560

②   85,107,639,472
    − 47,069,185,243

③   6,891,246,505
    − 2,888,666,111

④   9,659,241,378
    − 7,130,846,075

⑤   91,581,246,354
    − 4,488,671,243

⑥   72,369,821,456
    −   863,457,910

⑦   8,132,456,789
    − 4,676,330,458

⑧   97,799,862,134
    − 51,976,028,345

⑨   19,248,666,777
    − 6,243,970,581

Problems 10-18: *Round each number to the nearest <u>tenth of a trillion</u>, then subtract.*

⑩   8,026,586,241,351
    − 2,721,387,695,438

⑪   5,621,847,009,625
    − 4,963,241,890,250

⑫   24,310,678,921,592
    − 17,810,365,421,842

⑬   91,469,459,812,357
    − 77,289,392,604,526

⑭   58,261,371,802,156
    − 36,430,241,891,268

⑮   7,248,824,631,987
    − 1,971,632,832,456

⑯   62,729,326,585,241
    − 5,670,076,814,543

⑰   86,912,452,603,111
    − 77,802,462,315,810

⑱   41,960,281,342,619
    − 9,402,867,241,334

© Libro Studio LLC 2020

Name: _____

Score:

Problems 1-9: *Round each number to the nearest <u>tenth of a billion</u>, then subtract.*

①   37,862,591,246
   −34,298,761,245

②   52,498,160,891
   −44,730,621,581

③   8,976,431,248
   −6,859,321,487

④   93,249,862,980
   −18,026,875,245

⑤   61,634,521,809
   − 2,103,459,780

⑥   6,589,321,086
   −5,431,672,895

⑦   76,281,307,286
   −   754,689,150

⑧   66,375,981,646
   −48,976,312,834

⑨   80,679,281,391
   − 5,029,346,581

Problems 10-18: *Round each number to the nearest <u>tenth of a trillion</u>, then subtract.*

⑩   6,540,893,260,897
   −2,971,608,438,178

⑪   66,248,145,261,765
   −33,867,201,569,240

⑫   3,156,892,576,324
   −1,067,456,789,368

⑬   70,901,862,457,251
   − 7,013,467,824,919

⑭   84,751,021,602,561
   −31,072,341,867,259

⑮   71,361,289,567,689
   − 6,476,210,163,489

⑯   52,506,289,196,249
   −13,506,289,196,249

⑰   9,815,246,018,860
   −2,968,432,108,636

⑱   44,789,246,178,281
   − 2,712,346,289,563

© Libro Studio LLC 2020

Name: _____

Score:

Problems 1-6: *Round each number to the nearest <u>tenth of a billion</u>, then add.*

①   26,701,396,735
     8,246,359,728
+ 39,268,143,875

②   7,346,792,510
  69,935,428,367
+   861,021,578

③   5,502,861,341
   8,961,281,502
+ 6,791,486,024

④   7,268,143,875
  45,821,720,650
+ 6,872,132,879

⑤   6,389,500,286
  12,862,150,241
+ 57,632,154,872

⑥   9,728,821,543
  91,867,915,246
+ 5,249,689,671

Problems 7-12: *Round each number to the nearest <u>tenth of a trillion</u>, then add.*

⑦   37,269,385,620,130
    8,720,031,621,519
+ 91,000,689,241,932

⑧   1,901,861,249,565
   5,189,624,390,562
+ 7,972,347,621,987

⑨   51,423,167,389,026
    6,214,750,093,158
+   731,452,972,626

⑩   27,269,894,245,679
  49,381,246,721,542
+ 15,245,610,397,858

⑪   7,639,400,200,863
  26,902,089,561,249
+ 80,152,678,945,020

⑫   3,624,935,268,149
   9,635,432,154,526
+ 5,624,935,268,149

© Libro Studio LLC 2020

Name: _____

Problems 1-4: *Round each number to the nearest <u>ten</u>, then solve.*

① Eric rides the bus to school. The ride to school usually takes about 17 minutes. The ride home is usually 22 minutes. Roughly how much time does Eric spend on the bus each day?

② Amelia picked 34 apples, Jered picked 58 apples, and Ivy picked 41 apples. Roughly how many apples did they pick all together?

③ There are 153 students attending school 89 of them are girls. Approximately how many boys are there?

④ Elise is 9 years old. Her grandmother is 77. Approximately how much older is Elise's grandmother than Elise?

© Libro Studio LLC 2020

Name: _____

Score:

Problems 1-4: *Round each number to the nearest <u>hundred</u>, then solve.*

① A farmer had 822 chickens, then she sold 315 of them. Approximately how many chickens does she have left.

② Leo and Jacob are playing a video game. Leo currently has 1164 points. Jacob has 1977 points. Estimate how many more points Leo will need to score to catch up to Jacob.

③ Ava's restaurant served 708 people today, 630 people yesterday, and 785 people the day before that. Approximately how many people did the restaurant serve during these three days?

④ There are 318 pages in Freddie's book. He has already read 94 pages. Roughly how many pages does he still need to read?

© Libro Studio LLC 2020

Problems 1-4: *Round each number to the nearest __thousand__, then solve.*

① An elephant weights 6,327 kg. A killer whale weighs 5,168 kg. Roughly how much heavier is the elephant?

② There are 975 students in a school. The principal wants to get each student three pieces of candy for doing such a good job this year. Approximately how many pieces of candy will that be in total?

③ Sophia does clean her email inbox very often. She had 13,290 emails. She decided to delete 9,153 of the oldest emails. Approximately how many emails does she have left?

④ Records from the city hospital show that 4,732 babies were born there this year, 4,893 were born there last year and 4,481 were born there the year before that. Roughly how many babies were born at the hospital during these last three years?

© Libro Studio LLC 2020

Name: _____

Score:

Problems 1-4: *Round each number to the nearest <u>thousand</u>, then solve.*

① A factory made 43,471 chairs last year. This year it made 56,317 chairs. Approximately how many chairs did the factory make during these past two years?

② 14,529 people visited Oliver's his website this month. 29,602 people have visited Lily's website this month. About how many more visitors did Lily's website receive?

③ Kelsey loves photography. She has taken 6,831 pictures with her camera this year. Not all of the pictures turned out well. She decided to delete 4,107 of the pictures. Roughly, how many pictures does she still have?

④ David's café served 3,276 coffees on Thursday, 4,351 coffees on Friday, 3,591 coffees on Saturday, and 4,179 coffees Sunday. Approximately how many coffees did his café serve during these four days?

© Libro Studio LLC 2020

Name: _____

Score:

Problems 1-4: *Round each number to the nearest <u>ten thousand</u>, then solve.*

① 137,018 people live in the city of Kayport. Millington has a population of 80,941. Roughly how many more people live in Kayport?

② Rory likes to post funny videos online. His most popular video has been viewed 486,153 times. His second most popular video has been viewed 122,695 times. Approximately how many more views has his most popular video received?

③ The train station sold 40,368 tickets last year and 36,841 tickets the year before that. Approximately how many tickets did the station sell all together?

④ A king had 27,482 gold coins and 64,239 silver coins. That's roughly how many coins all together?

© Libro Studio LLC 2020

Name: _____

Score:

Problems 1-4: *Round each number to the nearest <u>hundred thousand</u>, then solve.*

① A television station says that an average broadcast of a football game will receive 329,125 viewers, but last year's championship game had 741,963 viewers. How many more people watched the championship game than the average football broadcast?

② Customers from a grocery store used 1,283,394 plastic shopping bags last year. This year the grocery store put up signs explaining the environmental benefits of reusable shopping bags and people only used 787,302 plastic shopping bags. How many fewer plastic shopping bags were used this year?

③ A city is trying to decide what to name its new bridge. Officials asked the citizens to go online and vote for the name they like most. "Oak Bridge" received 87,512 votes, "Grand Bridge" received 519,458 votes, and "Bridge of Dawn" received 294,186 votes. Roughly how many people voted all together.

④ The high score for a computer game is 623,738 points. Sarah scored 516,212 points. Approximately how many more points would she need to get the high score?

© Libro Studio LLC 2020

Name: _____

Score:

Problems 1-4: *Round each number to the nearest _million_, then solve.*

① Tokyo has a population of 37,464,174 people and Shanghai has a population of 26,354,728 people. Estimate how many more people live in Tokyo than Shanghai.

② A crayon factor made 56,313,753 crayons last year and 48,952,146 crayons last year. Approximately how many crayons is that all together?

③ The same crayon factory made 7,051,482 blue crayons, but only 2,170,520 tan crayons. Roughly how many more blue crayons were made than tan?

④ The factory made 4,624,869 green crayons, 6,413,843 red crayons, and 5,863,007 yellow crayons. Estimate how many green, red, and yellow crayons were made all together.

© Libro Studio LLC 2020

Name: _____

Score:

Problems 1-4: *Round each number to the nearest tenth of a million, then solve.*

① 75,299,518 cars were sold around the world last year. This year 78,426,905 were sold. How many more cars were sold this year than last year?

② If 66,674,983 people live in the United Kingdom and 24,985,746 people live in Australia, roughly how many more people live in the United Kingdom than Australia?

③ If 5,429,524 people live in Toronto, 3,519,595 people live in Montreal, and 2,264,823 people live in Vancouver, then approximately how many people live in these three cities combined?

④ 15,171,978 plane tickets were sold at the airport last year and 16,808,672 tickets were sold this year. Approximately how many more tickets were sold this year than last year?

© Libro Studio LLC 2020

Name: _____

Score:

Problems 1-4: *Round each number to the nearest _million_, then solve.*

1. If about 24.99 million people live in Australia and about 4.89 million people live in New Zealand, approximately how many more people live in Australia than New Zealand?

2. Studies estimate that 37.9 million trees grew in a forest a decade ago. Since then 6.28 million trees have be cut down in this forest. Estimate how many trees are left.

3. A hospital added a new medical wing to its building. It cost the hospital 11.3 million to build and 5.8 million to purchase the beds and medical equipment needed for the new wing. How much money did the hospital spend?

4. An earthquake has left millions of people without food, water, or electricity. People from around the world have been donating items to help these people. 4.2 million cans of food and 6.9 million bottles of water have been donated so far. Roughly how many items is this all together?

© Libro Studio LLC 2020

Name: _____

Score:

Problems 1-4: *Round each number to the nearest whole number, then solve.*

① A skyscraper used about 12.7 gigawatts of electricity each day last year. This year the rooms were updated with more energy efficient light bulbs and the skyscraper only used about 9.8 gigawatts of electricity each day. Roughly how many gigawatts of electricity did the new light bulbs save?

② Mike had 57.05 gigabytes of space left on his computer before downloading some new computer games. Now his computer only has 15.93 gigabytes of space. How much space did the new games use?

③ Mike decides that he wants his computer to have more than 15.93 gigabytes of space. He deletes two old computer game that he does not use any more. One game was 5.73 gigabytes and the other 26.18 gigabytes. Approximately how many gigabytes of open space does his computer have now?

④ Rachel ran a race in 35.19 seconds. Ava ran the race in 29.84 seconds. Approximately how much faster was Ava?

© Libro Studio LLC 2020

Answers

Day 1:
1) 8, 6 2) 4, 9 3) 1, 1 4) 0, 8 5) 2, 7
6) 9, 3 7) 3, 5 8) 7, 7 9) 5, 4 10) 6, 0
11) 70 12) 40 13) 40 14) 20 15) 60
16) 90 17) 20 18) 10 19) 90 20) 50

Day 2:
1) 40 2) 6 3) 8 4) 80 5) 0
6) 20 7) 7 8) 10 9) 0 10) 90
11) 40 + 5 12) 20 + 7 13) 50 + 1 14) 90 + 0
15) 30 + 6 16) 10 + 8 17) 60 + 0 18) 70 + 3
19) 5 20) 80 + 4 21) 79 22) 53 23) 85 24) 12 25) 66
26) 21 27) 90 28) 48 29) 34 30) 16

Day 3:
1) 80 2) 50 3) 30 4) 10 5) 70
6) 10 7) 30 8) 80 9) 90 10) 90
11) 90 12) 20 13) 20 14) 90 15) 50

Day 4:
1) 50 2) 80 3) 30 4) 30 5) 0
6) 90 7) 60 8) 20 9) 80 10) 100
11) 40 12) 10 13) 30 14) 10 15) 20
16) 80 17) 50 18) 90 19) 60 20) 50
21) 80 22) 0 23) 20 24) 30 25) 80
26) 50 27) 60 28) 40 29) 20 30) 20
31) 100 32) 60 33) 10 34) 90 35) 30
36) 50 37) 70 38) 30 39) 90 40) 10

Day 5:
1) 40 2) 20 3) 70 4) 90 5) 40
6) 60 7) 100 8) 10 9) 10 10) 20
11) 60 12) 90 13) 70 14) 90 15) 110
16) 80 17) 90 18) 170 19) 140 20) 40
21) 60 22) 70 23) 100 24) 90 25) 60
26) 70 27) 130 28) 170 29) 70 30) 60

Day 6:
1) 1, 8, 6 2) 4, 1, 0 3) 7, 2, 3 4) 9, 0, 5 5) 0, 9, 7
6) 700 7) 200 8) 400 9) 300 10) 100
11) 300 12) 800 13) 500 14) 1,000 15) 0

Day 7:
1) 400 2) 6 3) 80 4) 800 5) 0
6) 20 7) 700 8) 60 9) 7 10) 900
11) 300 + 60 + 5 12) 400 + 20 + 7
13) 600 + 80 + 9 14) 100 + 60 + 4
15) 800 + 50 + 3 16) 500 + 70 +2
17) 900 + 30 + 1 18) 200 + 0 + 8
19) 400 + 50 + 0 20) 700 + 90 +7
21) 679 22) 712 23) 155 24) 403 25) 391
26) 580 27) 236 28) 974 29) 111 30) 489

Day 8:
1) 900 2) 500 3) 300 4) 700 5) 100
6) 700 7) 200 8) 0 9) 800 10) 200
11) 500 12) 1,000 13) 100 14) 900 15) 300

Day 9:
1) 500 2) 400 3) 700 4) 100 5) 400 6) 300
7) 800 8) 400 9) 800 10) 1,000 11) 100 12) 700
13) 900 14) 100 15) 600 16) 200 17) 500 18) 200
19) 400 20) 800

21) 500 22) 700 23) 800 24) 200 25) 300 26) 700
27) 400 28) 200 29) 600 30) 100 31) 1,000 32) 600
33) 900 34) 700 35) 500 36) 500 37) 300 38) 100
39) 300 40) 600

Day 10:
1) 200 2) 500 3) 900 4) 0 5) 900
6) 300 7) 100 8) 300 9) 400 10) 700
11 400 12) 1,000 13) 1,200 14) 1,700
15) 1,700 16) 800 17) 1,100 18) 1,000
19) 1,000 20) 800 21) 1,200 22) 1,700
23) 1,200 24) 1,500 25) 900 26) 1,100
27) 1,100 28) 1,300 29) 1,100 30) 900

Day 11:
1) 680 2) 180 3) 430 4) 400 5) 100
6) 260 7) 850 8) 510 9) 950 10) 40
11) 80 12) 380 13) 650 14) 120 15) 600
16) 710 17) 230 18) 900 19) 470 20) 680

Day 12:
1) 200, 190 2) 400, 410 3) 700, 720
4) 900, 910 5) 100, 90 6) 300, 350
7) 900, 880 8) 200, 200 9) 600, 560
10) 100, 100 11) 600, 650 12) 1,000, 960
13) 0, 30 14) 300, 320 15) 800, 800

Day 13:
1) 1,100 2) 800 3) 1,200 4) 1,500
5) 600 6) 1,000 7) 1,100 8) 1,200
9) 1,000 10) 800 11) 1,300 12) 1,600
13) 1,070 14) 630 15) 1,280 16) 1,060
17) 730 18) 960 19) 1,500 20) 740
21) 1,160 22) 1,490 23) 1,270 24) 830

Day 14:
1) 3, 0, 1, 6 2) 9, 4, 2, 5 3) 7, 1, 7, 8 4) 5, 9, 0, 5
5) 1, 2, 3, 7
6) 1,000 7) 8,000 8) 2,000 9) 6,000 10) 1,000
11) 4,000 12) 7,000 13) 4,000 14) 0 15) 10,000

Day 15:
1) 4,000 2) 50 3) 800 4) 8,000 5) 1
6) 2,000 7) 8 8) 1,000 9) 60 10) 9,000
11) 1,000 + 800 + 30 + 5
12) 5,000 + 800 + 20 + 1
13) 7,000 + 400 + 60 + 2
14) 3,000 + 900 + 90
15) 6,000 + 40 + 5
16) 6,463 17) 1,527 18) 3,099 19) 7,284 20) 9,400

Day 16:
1) 7,000 2) 6,000 3) 2,000 4) 10,000 5) 3,000
6) 3,000 7) 0 8) 7,000 9) 8,000 10) 5,000
11) 1,000 12) 5,000 13) 8,000 14) 1,000 15) 3,000

Day 17:
1) 1,000 2) 8,000 3) 4,000 4) 9,000 5) 6,000
6) 2,000 7) 8,000 8) 5,000 9) 7,000 10) 1,000
11) 2,000 12) 3,000 13) 4,000 14) 5,000 15) 6,000
16) 8,000 17) 3,000 18) 9,000 19) 10,000 20) 1,000
21) 3,000 22) 5,000 23) 6,000 24) 7,000 25) 7,000
26) 8,000 27) 9,000 28) 2,000 29) 4,000 30) 3,000
31) 5,000 32) 8,000 33) 6,000 34) 7,000 35) 6,000
36) 10,000 37) 4,000 38) 2,000 39) 2,000 40) 4,000

Day 18:
1) 3,000 2) 6,000 3) 8,000 4) 10,000 5) 2,000
6) 5,000 7) 1,000 8) 6,000 9) 9,000 10) 1,000
11) 7,000 12) 14,000 13) 17,000
14) 12,000 15) 9,000 16) 8,000
17) 6,000 18) 13,000 19) 11,000
20) 14,000 21) 9,000 22) 17,000
23) 13,000 24) 10,000 25) 10,000

Day 19:
1) 6,000, 6,300, 6,300 2) 1,000, 1,500, 1,450
3) 9,000, 8,900, 8,910 4) 4,000, 4,300, 4,260
5) 7,000, 6,500, 6,520 6) 3,000, 2,900, 2,890
7) 6,000, 5,700, 5,710 8) 2,000, 2,000, 1,970
9) 4,000, 3,500, 3,530 10) 2,000, 2,500, 2,460
11) 10,000, 9,600, 9,640 12) 4,000, 3,900, 3,900
13) 5,000, 5,300, 5,320 14) 3,000, 3,500, 3,500
15) 7,000, 7,100, 7,100

Day 20:
1) 2,000 2) 4,000 3) 7,000 4) 9,000 5) 2,000
6) 2,000 7) 3,000 8) 6,000 9) 9,000 10) 1,000
11) 9,000 12) 1,000 13) 7,000 14) 2,000 15) 8,000
16) 5,000 17) 10,000 18) 3,000 19) 8,000 20) 5,000
21) 3,000 22) 2,700 23) 5,100 24) 7,9
00 25) 1,500
26) 8,400 27) 4,700 28) 6,500 29) 3,800 30) 9,100
31) 1,300 32) 3,100 33) 1,400 34) 4,700 35) 5,100
36) 6,400 37) 7,000 38) 2,700 39) 10,000 40) 8,400

Day 21:
1) 9,000, 9,400, 9,420 2) 7,000, 6,600, 6,590
3) 1,000, 1,100, 1,080 4) 4,000, 4,400, 4,350
5) 6,000, 6,000, 5,980 6) 3,000, 2,800, 2,850
7) 4,000, 4,100, 4,070 8) 1,000, 1,300, 1,340
9) 3,000, 3,300, 3,250 10) 7,000, 6,700, 6,700
11) 5,000, 5,400, 5,420 12) 9,000, 8,900, 8,910
13) 2,000, 2,200, 2,180 14) 7,000, 7,000, 7,020
15) 4,000, 3,600, 3,590

Day 22:
1) 4,000 2) 8,000 3) 1,000 4) 10,000 5) 5,000
6) 3,000 7) 8,000 8) 4,000 9) 5,000 10) 10,000
11) 8,000 12) 1,000 13) 7,000 14) 9,000 15) 7,000
16) 9,000 17) 5,000 18) 3,000 19) 6,000 20) 4,000
21) 1,600 22) 6,000 23) 9,600 24) 4,200 25) 9,400
26) 1,300 27) 2,600 28) 3,900 29) 8,000 30) 4,800
31) 9,700 32) 5,300 33) 1,300 34) 6,100 35) 6,800
36) 8,400 37) 7,300 38) 3,900 39) 7,900 40) 2,600

Day 23:
1) 6,000, 6,400, 6,390 2) 3,000, 2,600, 2,600
3) 1,000, 1,100, 1,100 4) 5,000, 5,300, 5,300
5) 7,000, 7,400, 7,440 6) 10,000, 9,700, 9,730
7) 5,000, 5,000, 4,980 8) 7,000, 6,800, 6,810
9) 6,000, 5,700, 5,720 10) 4,000, 4,100, 4,090
11) 2,000, 2,500, 2,500 12) 7,000, 7,300, 7,260
13) 4,000, 3,800, 3,810 14) 8,000, 8,300, 8,350
15) 3,000, 3,100, 3,130

Day 24:
1) 9,000 2) 5,000 3) 9,000 4) 3,000 5) 2,000
6) 7,000 7) 2,000 8) 7,000 9) 3,000 10) 7,000
11) 2,000 12) 9,000 13) 6,000 14) 2,000 15) 6,000
16) 9,000 17) 8,000 18) 4,000 19) 10,000 20) 6,000
21) 2,600 22) 6,400 23) 1,000 24) 5,900 25) 4,200
26) 2,900 27) 2,300 28) 4,000 29) 8,000 30) 9,500
31) 7,900 32) 7,300 33) 1,700 34) 4,900 35) 5,200
36) 8,300 37) 3,200 38) 6,900 39) 9,600 40) 1,800

© Libro Studio LLC 2020

Answers

Day 25:
1) 17,000 2) 7,000 3) 14,000
4) 12,000 5) 6,000 6) 15,000
7) 5,000 8) 14,000 9) 7,000
10) 6,100 11) 17,800 12) 10,400
13) 15,200 14) 4,400 15) 8,800
16) 10,800 17) 13,900 18) 10,900

Day 26:
1) 5,000 2) 17,000 3) 14,000
4) 7,000 5) 11,000 6) 12,000
7) 8,000 8) 15,000 9) 10,000
10) 3,600 11) 16,200 12) 8,100
13) 14,000 14) 12,100 15) 11,400
16) 9,000 17) 7,700 18) 17,300

Day 27:
1) 5,000 2) 2,000 3) 6,000
4) 1,000 5) 8,000 6) 4,000
7) 2,000 8) 6,000 9) 2,000
10) 2,100 11) 5,500 12) 1,400
13) 3,900 14) 3,400 15) 900
16) 1,200 17) 3,600 18) 2,200

Day 28:
1) 4,000 2) 1,000 3) 5,000
4) 2,000 5) 1,000 6) 3,000
7) 4,000 8) 1,000 9) 0
10) 2,900 11) 1,100 12) 400
13) 6,000 14) 2,200 15) 600
16) 300 17) 4,200 18) 900

Day 29:
1) 17,000 2) 16,000 3) 20,000
4) 19,000 5) 13,000 6) 14,000
7) 15,000 8) 17,000 9) 22,000
10) 13,000 11) 16,000 12) 16,000

Day 30:
1) 14,000 2) 15,000 3) 14,000
4) 17,000 5) 24,000 6) 14,000
7) 14,000 8) 16,000 9) 12,000
10) 15,000 11) 18,000 12) 23,000

Day 31:
1) 40,000, forty thousand
2) 800,000, eight hundred thousand
3) 8,000,000, eight million
4) 80,000, eighty thousand
5) 8,000, eight thousand
6) 500,000, five hundred thousand
7) 1,000,000, one million
8) 5,000, five thousand
9) 30, thirty
10) 300, three hundred
11) 0, zero
12) 4,000,000, four million
13) 100, one hundred
14) 900,000, nine hundred thousand
15) 10, ten

Day 32:
1) 6,305,472 2) 2,467,931 3) 9,078,624
4) 1,928,653 5) 7,123,480 6) 5,270,689
7) 3,528,706 8) 6,892,317 9) 1,862,950
10) 4,820,175 11) 7,384,570 12) 2,734,590
13) 9,120,368 14) 8,795,652 15) 8,654,231

Day 33:
1) One million, six hundred twenty-nine thousand, one hundred seventy
2) One million, four hundred eighty-nine thousand, six hundred thirty-seven
3) Three million, seventy-two thousand, one hundred thirty-six
4) Eight million, five hundred twenty-three thousand, six hundred seventy-four
5) Four million, six hundred seventy-three thousand, nine hundred fifty
6) Nine million, seven hundred thousand, six hundred thirteen
7) Six million, eight hundred thirty-nine thousand, two hundred fifteen
8) Five million, three hundred forty-two thousand, nine hundred sixty-seven
9) Three million, two hundred six thousand, five hundred ninety-one
10) Four million, seven hundred thirty-two thousand, eight hundred fifteen
11) Two million, one hundred fifty-four thousand, seven hundred eighty-nine
12) Seven million, twelve thousand, three hundred seventy-eight

Day 34:
1) 9,000,000, 9,000,000, 9,040,000
2) 7,000,000, 6,500,000, 6,530,000
3) 7,000,000, 7,400,000, 7,410,000
4) 4,000,000, 3,700,000, 3,680,000
5) 2,000,000, 1,900,000, 1,870,000
6) 10,000,000, 9,700,000, 9,650,000
7) 4,000,000, 4,200,000, 4,240,000
8) 7,000,000, 6,900,000, 6,890,000
9) 2,000,000, 2,000,000, 2,040,000
10) 6,000,000, 5,700,000, 5,720,000
11) 8,000,000, 7,900,000, 7,940,000
12) 3,000,000, 3,500,000, 3,460,000
13) 5,000,000, 4,600,000, 4,600,000
14) 8,000,000, 8,400,000, 8,390,000
15) 5,000,000, 5,200,000, 5,190,000

Day 35:
1) 4,000,000 2) 9,000,000 3) 6,000,000
4) 4,000,000 5) 3,000,000 6) 8,000,000
7) 2,000,000 8) 10,000,000 9) 5,000,000
10) 9,000,000 11) 4,000,000 12) 2,000,000
13) 5,000,000 14) 2,000,000 15) 8,000,000
16) 5,000,000 17) 6,800,000 18) 1,400,000
19) 5,800,000 20) 8,100,000 21) 7,600,000
22) 4,600,000 23) 7,100,000 24) 3,000,000
25) 1,400,000 26) 9,300,000 27) 6,400,000
28) 3,000,000 29) 9,500,000 30) 2,500,000
31) 3,700,000 32) 8,300,000

Day 36:
1) 9,000,000, 9,000,000, 9,040,000
2) 9,000,000, 8,900,000, 8,860,000
3) 6,000,000, 6,300,000, 6,320,000
4) 2,000,000, 1,700,000, 1,750,000
5) 5,000,000, 4,900,000, 4,920,000
6) 5,000,000, 5,100,000, 5,070,000
7) 7,000,000, 7,400,000, 7,430,000
8) 3,000,000, 2,600,000, 2,610,000
9) 5,000,000, 5,200,000, 5,230,000
10) 7,000,000, 6,600,000, 6,570,000
11) 4,000,000, 3,600,000, 3,610,000
12) 9,000,000, 9,400,000, 9,410,000
13) 7,000,000, 7,200,000, 7,190,000
14) 4,000,000, 4,400,000, 4,370,000
15) 9,000,000, 8,600,000, 8,580,000

Day 37:
1) 1,000,000 2) 10,000,000 3) 3,000,000
4) 6,000,000 5) 10,000,000 6) 4,000,000
7) 6,000,000 8) 2,000,000 9) 2,000,000
10) 4,000,000 11) 7,000,000 12) 5,000,000
13) 6,000,000 14) 8,000,000 15) 3,000,000
16) 4,000,000 17) 4,400,000 18) 8,700,000
19) 1,500,000 20) 3,700,000 21) 10,00,000
22) 5,800,000 23) 6,300,000 24) 6,200,000
25) 3,200,000 26) 1,900,000 27) 7,100,000
28) 2,400,000 29) 8,700,000 30) 9,300,000
31) 3,000,000 32) 7,300,000

Day 38:
1) 9,000,000, 9,000,000, 9,040,000
2) 7,000,000, 6,900,000, 6,930,000
3) 2,000,000, 1,700,000, 1,740,000
4) 5,000,000, 5,200,000, 5,190,000
5) 7,000,000, 7,000,000, 7,010,000
6) 3,000,000, 2,700,000, 2,680,000
7) 6,000,000, 6,300,000, 6,330,000
8) 5,000,000, 4,700,000, 4,740,000
9) 8,000,000, 8,400,000, 8,370,000
10) 3,000,000, 3,300,000, 3,300,000
11) 8,000,000, 7,800,000, 7,800,000
12) 5,000,000, 5,200,000, 5,160,000
13) 10,000,000, 9,600,000, 9,550,000
14) 4,000,000, 4,400,000, 4,430,000
15) 8,000,000, 8,400,000, 8,370,000

Day 39:
1) 11,000,000 2) 8,000,000 3) 13,000,000
4) 16,000,000 5) 6,000,000 6) 10,000,000
7) 7,400,000 8) 11,700,000 9) 11,100,000
10) 10,200,000 11) 12,900,000 12) 10,600,000

Day 40:
1) 15,000,000 2) 10,000,000 3) 17,000,000
4) 10,000,000 5) 9,000,000 6) 12,000,000
7) 8,400,000 8) 4,900,000 9) 15,200,000
10) 10,100,000 11) 13,400,000 12) 11,700,000

Day 41:
1) 3,000,000 2) 2,000,000 3) 4,000,000
4) 5,000,000 5) 5,000,000 6) 1,000,000
7) 5,500,000 8) 1,200,000 9) 2,100,000
10) 2,000,000 11) 1,100,000 12) 1,200,000

Day 42:
1) 0 2) 1,000,000 3) 2,000,000
4) 7,000,000 5) 4,000,000 6) 4,000,000
7) 3,000,000 8) 3,200,000 9) 5,200,000
10) 1,500,000 11) 700,000 12) 1,100,000

© Libro Studio LLC 2020

Answers

Day 43:
1) 13,000,000 2) 17,000,000 3) 19,000,000
4) 16,000,000 5) 11,000,000 6) 14,000,000
7) 20,000,000 8) 17,000,000 9) 13,000,000
10) 19,000,000 11) 24,000,000 12) 16,000,000

Day 44:
1) 16,000,000 2) 15,000,000 3) 17,000,000
4) 13,000,000 5) 22,000,000 6) 13,000,000
7) 20,000,000 8) 11,000,000 9) 20,000,000
10) 22,000,000 11) 14,000,000 12) 13,000,000

Day 45:
1) 0.7, seven tenths
2) 7, seven
3) 0.009, nine thousandths
4) 0.5, five tenths
5) 3, three
6) 0.001, one thousandth
7) 0.07, seven hundredths
8) 7, seven
9) 50, fifty
10) 0.9, nine tenths
11) 6, six
12) 0.05, five hundredths

Day 46:
1) 61.027 2) 75.934 3) 501.61
4) 48.297 5) 50.824 6) 27.419
7) 97.235 8) 0.49 9) 27.385
10) 73.804 11) 386.20 12) 824.50
13) 469.81 14) 614.52 15) 346.28

Day 47:
1) One hundred seventy-four and thirty-eight hundredths
2) Five hundred seventy-three and forty-nine hundredths
3) Nine hundred eight and seventy-seven hundredths
4) Fifty-four and one hundred twenty-six thousandths
5) Sixty-one and three hundred five thousandths
6) Zero and four hundred twenty thousandths
7) Six hundred seventy-two and forty-three hundredths
8) Seven hundred thirty-four and sixty-two hundredths
9) Two hundred sixty-nine and eighty-three hundredths
10) Eighty-four and two hundred ninety-one thousandths
11) Thirty-one and eight hundred sixty-four thousandths
12) Four hundred twenty and seventeen hundredths

Day 48:
1) 20, 19.5, 19.52 2) 105, 104.9, 104.87
3) 7, 7.1, 7.07 4) 97, 97.4, 97.39
5) 1, 0.9, 0.85 6) 28, 28.0, 28.05
7) 82, 81.6, 81.58 8) 4, 4.0, 3.99
9) 703, 703.3, 703.26 10) 9, 8.60, 8.65
11) 176, 176.4, 176.41 12) 430, 430.1, 430.13
13) 10, 9.8, 9.78 14) 0, 0.2, 0.17
15) 50, 50.0, 50.04

Day 49:
1) 5 2) 13 3) 10 4) 0
5) 1 6) 935 7) 24 8) 5
9) 7 10) 381 11) 89 12) 420
13) 60 14) 0 15) 341 16) 49
17) 738.1 18) 8.2 19) 439.8 20) 97.7
21) 12.4 22) 8.3 23) 75 24) 6.9
25) 5.8 26) 705.3 27) 0.1 28) 5.8
29) 2.4 30) 3.6 31) 69.5 32) 12.3

Day 50:
1) 1, 1.4, 1.39
2) 88, 87.6, 87.61
3) 302, 301.6, 301.57
4) 815, 815.0, 815.04
5) 6, 6.5, 6.49
6) 735, 734.9, 734.89
7) 1, 0.8, 0.76
8) 281, 281.3, 281.35
9) 2, 1.6, 1.57
10) 429, 428.9, 428.91
11) 9, 9.5, 9.48
12) 0, 0.2, 0.23
13) 5, 4.7, 4.67
14) 601, 601.0, 601.03
15) 6, 5.7, 5.70

Day 51:
1) 5 2) 13 3) 10 4) 0
5) 35 6) 82 7) 7 8) 6
9) 613 10) 967 11) 0 12) 97
13) 1 14) 25 15) 7 16) 5
17) 0.3 18) 3.9 19) 209.9 20) 0.1
21) 367.7 22) 0.4 23) 978.6 24) 1.6
25) 2.3 26) 556.3 27) 6.3 28) 5.3
29) 4.7 30) 4.8 31) 618.1 32) 1.7

Day 52:
1) 23 2) 390 3) 9
4) 525 5) 14 6) 138
7) 92 8) 803 9) 7
10) 273.4 11) 738.9 12) 89.3
13) 743.2 14) 7.3 15) 424.1
16) 8.7 17) 13.3 18) 6.4

Day 53:
1) 13 2) 4 3) 296
4) 6 5) 321 6) 433
7) 4 8) 4 9) 3
10) 4.1 11) 5.4 12) 0.3
13) 286.5 14) 12 15) 21.5
16) 630.5 17) 2.6 18) 145.9

Day 54:
1) 36 2) 11
3) 794 4) 685
5) 759 6) 19
7) 173 8) 1,242
9) 253 10) 20
11) 9 12) 453

Day 55:
1) 3.7 million, Three point seven million
2) 48.6 million, Forty-eight point six million
3) 6.3 million, Six point three million
4) 5.1 million, Five point one million
5) 27.3 million, Twenty-seven point three million
6) 9.3 million, Nine point three million
7) 82.5 million, Eighty-two point five million
8) 46.7 million, Forty-six point seven million
9) 3.2 million, Three point two million
10) 60.4 million, Sixty point four million
11) 93.6 million, Ninety-three point six million
12) 7.1 million, Seven point one million
13) 9.9 million, Nine point nine million
14) 1.8 million, One point eight million
15) 76.6 million, Seventy-six point six million

Day 56:
1) 238.6 million
2) 50.1 million
3) 3.5 million
4) 139.2 million
5) 6.1 million
6) 9.7 million
7) 43.9 million
8) 13.8 million
9) 78.5 million
10) 2.3 million
11) 257.6 million
12) 87.6 million
13) 3.2 million
14) 507.4 million
15) 864.7 million

Day 57:
1) 9.073857 million, 9.1 million
2) 1.789204 million, 1.8 million
3) 3.958612 million, 4 million
4) 7.402693 million, 7.4 million
5) 3.015678 million, 3.0 million
6) 6.392851 million, 6.4 million
7) 9.250136 million, 9.3 million
8) 6.843751 million, 6.8 million
9) 4.931025 million, 4.9 million
10) 8.174639 million, 8.2 million
11) 2.369780 million, 2.4 million
12) 5.382019 million, 5.4 million
13) 7.924308 million, 7.9 million
14) 4.019827 million, 4.0 million
15) 5.704180 million, 5.7 million

Day 58:
1) 17.8 million, Seventeen point eight million
2) 7.9 million, Seven point nine million
3) 8.6 million, Eight point six million
4) 28 million, Twenty-eight million
5) 52.7 million, Fifty-two point seven million
6) 85.3 million, Eighty-five point three million
7) 97.4 million, Ninety-seven point four million
8) 6.5 million, Six point five million
9) 31.3 million, Thirty-one point three million
10) 90.7 million, Ninety point seven million
11) 1.8 million, One point eight million
12) 4.4 million, Four point four million
13) 79.0 million, Seventy-nine point zero million
14) 10.6 million, Ten point six million
15) 2.2 million, Two point two million

© Libro Studio LLC 2020

Answers

Day 59:
1) 17.8 million 2) 4.2 million 3) 1.6 million
4) 57.5 million 5) 2.8 million 6) 18.4 million
7) 3.3 million 8) 4 million 9) 45.1 million
10) 6.1 million 11) 6.4 million 12) 92.2 million
13) 8.3 million 14) 3.7 million 15) 79.9 million
16) 6 million 17) 2.1 million 18) 5.9 million
19) 28.3 million 20) 30.6 million 21) 7.5 million
22) 44.4 million 23) 2 million 24) 51.8 million
25) 81.2 million 26) 4.5 million 27) 9.2 million
28) 3.8 million 29) 6.1 million 30) 31 million
31) 9.7 million 32) 26.5 million

Day 60:
1) 0.873857 million, 0.8 million
2) 6.201867 million, 6.2 million
3) 9.724589 million, 9.7 million
4) 0.920657 million, 0.9 million
5) 36.821073 million, 36.8 million
6) 9.023486 million, 9.0 million
7) 7.453492 million, 7.5 million
8) 11.980436 million, 12 million
9) 4.365497 million, 4.4 million
10) 87.138546 million, 87.1 million
11) 1.624794 million, 1.6 million
12) 8.634281 million, 8.6 million
13) 12.532408 million, 12.5 million
14) 58.428391 million, 58.4 million
15) 0.792419 million, 0.8 million

Day 61:
1) 11.2 million 2) 15.7 million
3) 11.8 million 4) 52.8 million
5) 11.4 million 6) 36.3 million
7) 77.9 million 8) 15.8 million
9) 3.4 million 10) 47.5 million
11) 68.2 million 12) 13.5 million
13) 79.8 million 14) 76.4 million

Day 62:
1) 62.6 million 2) 94.6 million
3) 10.8 million 4) 68.3 million
5) 8.7 million 6) 16.5 million
7) 49.3 million 8) 40.8 million
9) 80.4 million 10) 32.7 million
11) 53.5 million 12) 55.5 million
13) 11.3 million 14) 4.5 million

Day 63:
1) 22.9 million 2) 83.2 million
3) 30.5 million 4) 64.2 million
5) 29 million 6) 19.2 million
7) 16.9 million 8) 36.2 million
9) 83 million 10) 17.3 million
11) 13.3 million 12) 52.9 million

Day 64:
1) 16.1 million 2) 56.7 million
3) 53.5 million 4) 56.4 million
5) 13.5 million 6) 72.5 million
7) 75.9 million 8) 15.4 million
9) 17.3 million 10) 30.7 million
11) 89.1 million 12) 29.1 million

Day 65:
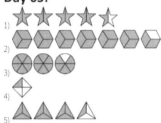
6) $3\frac{1}{2}$ 7) $7\frac{3}{4}$ 8) $1\frac{3}{8}$ 9) 6 10) $4\frac{2}{6}$

Day 66:
1) $13\frac{1}{3}$ 2) $6\frac{4}{9}$ 3) $1\frac{5}{6}$ 4) $7\frac{2}{3}$ 5) $34\frac{1}{2}$
6) $4\frac{7}{20}$ 7) $12\frac{3}{5}$ 8) $10\frac{13}{16}$ 9) $\frac{3}{4}$ 10) $8\frac{8}{25}$
11) Five and three-sevenths
12) Two and two-fifths
13) One and nine-tenths
14) Four-ninths
15) Four and one-half

Day 67:
1) 3 2) 9 3) 21 4) 1
5) 3 6) 15 7) 8 8) 6

Day 68:
1) 1 2) 17 3) 0 4) 10 5) 3
6) 13 7) 1 8) 6 9) 2 10) 4
11) 5 12) 28 13) 14 14) 4 15) 1

Day 69:
1) 8 2) 2 3) 9 4) 1 5) 1
6) 1 7) 23 8) 4 9) 4 10) 10
11) 0 12) 46 13) 6 14) 13 15) 7

Day 70:
1) 5 2) 8 3) 12 4) 0 5) 20
6) 51 7) 2 8) 9 9) 26 10) 7
11) 16 12) 1 13) 0 14) 3 15) 5
16) 34 17) 2 18) 1 19) 6 20) 4
21) 1 22) 2 23) 7 24) 12 25) 4
26) 8 27) 5 28) 34 29) 3 30) 1
31) 10 32) 4 33) 7 34) 1 35) 6
36) 15 37) 13 38) 22 39) 26 40) 11

Day 71:
1) 1 2) 3 3) 35 4) 1 5) 5
6) 21 7) 0 8) 12 9) 10 10) 5
11) 3 12) 7 13) 10 14) 8 15) 0
16) 54 17) 17 18) 1 19) 16 20) 14
21) 4 22) 10 23) 0 24) 3 25) 7
26) 9 27) 0 28) 2 29) 8 30) 3
31) 6 32) 44 33) 80 34) 12 35) 15
36) 1 37) 13 38) 33 39) 0 40) 27

Day 72:
1) 13 2) 3 3) 10 4) 3 5) 15
6) 5 7) 5 8) 0 9) 0 10) 6
11) 11 12) 23 13) 28 14) 8 15) 1
16) 14 17) 40 18) 80 19) 1 20) 7
21) 6 22) 11 23) 7 24) 4 25) 9
26) 76 27) 1 28) 13 29) 0 30) 8
31) 3 32) 2 33) 15 34) 1 35) 3
36) 12 37) 51 38) 84 39) 51 40) 7

Day 73:
1) 4 2) 7 3) 7 4) 1 5) 3
6) 0 7) 5 8) 100 9) 4 10) 0
11) 8 12) 25 13) 15 14) 31 15) 92
16) 53 17) 10 18) 6 19) 3 20) 1
21) 9 22) 15 23) 1 24) 0 25) 1
26) 10 27) 9 28) 23 29) 17 30) 36
31) 1 32) 0 33) 6 34) 8 35) 1
36) 3 37) 24 38) 63 39) 60 40) 2

Day 74:
1) 11 2) 0 3) 5 4) 10 5) 6
6) 8 7) 4 8) 1 9) 4 10) 0
11) 8 12) 11 13) 0 14) 28 15) 16
16) 14 17) 30 18) 13 19) 21 20) 18
21) 9 22) 1 23) 5 24) 2 25) 18
26) 10 27) 3 28) 0 29) 1 30) 7
31) 1 32) 41 33) 16 34) 9 35) 4
36) 18 37) 6 38) 50 39) 11 40) 1

Day 75:
1) 2 2) 9 3) 5 4) 2 5) 25
6) 20 7) 92 8) 0 9) 0 10) 9
11) 7 12) 3 13) 4 14) 7 15) 10
16) 0 17) 0 18) 12 19) 13 20) 13
21) 8 22) 2 23) 5 24) 7 25) 10
26) 2 27) 5 28) 9 29) 6 30) 3
31) 17 32) 22 33) 31 34) 3 35) 6
36) 7 37) 9 38) 27 39) 1 40) 1

Day 76:
1) 13 2) 17 3) 15
4) 12 5) 16 6) 5
7) 26 8) 5 9) 26
10) 16 11) 19 12) 9
13) 48 14) 10 15) 16
16) 14 17) 25 18) 13
19) 3 20) 14 21) 13
22) 15 23) 12 24) 17

Day 77:
1) 4 2) 12 3) 16
4) 9 5) 21 6) 24
7) 13 8) 22 9) 7
10) 11 11) 32 12) 32
13) 20 14) 17 15) 8
16) 16 17) 9 18) 31
19) 10 20) 17 21) 18
22) 21 23) 6 24) 12

Day 78:
1) 4 2) 10 3) 4
4) 11 5) 6 6) 11
7) 2 8) 7 9) 2
10) 8 11) 7 12) 11
13) 1 14) 4 15) 8
16) 1 17) 3 18) 2
19) 5 20) 5 21) 9
22) 2 23) 2 24) 1

Day 79:
1) 0 2) 6 3) 0
4) 2 5) 3 6) 2
7) 15 8) 1 9) 16
10) 3 11) 6 12) 5
13) 2 14) 3 15) 18
16) 1 17) 1 18) 9
19) 7 20) 3 21) 9
22) 3 23) 11 24) 7

© Libro Studio LLC 2020

Answers

Day 80:
1) 40,000,000,000,000, Forty trillion
2) 4,000,000,000, Four billion
3) 900,000,000,000,000, Nine hundred trillion
4) 200,000,000,000, Two hundred billion
5) 60,000,000,000,000, Sixty trillion
6) 7,000,000,000,000, Seven trillion
7) 6,000,000,000, Six billion
8) 50,000,000,000, Fifty billion
9) 10,000,000,000,000, Ten trillion
10) 200,000,000,000, Two hundred billion
11) 9,000,000,000,000, Nine trillion
12) 300,000,000,000, Three hundred billion
13) 6,000,000,000,000, Six trillion
14) 7,000,000,000,000, Seven trillion
15) 1,000,000,000, One billion

Day 81:
1) 32,603,584,966,114
2) 8,630,458,927,715
3) 47,000,000,085,394
4) 74,567,890,431,243
5) 10,283,745,690,980
6) 3,831,569,200,000
7) 20,913,756,824,732
8) 53,012,345,678,918
9) 86,107,543,218,601
10) 20,000,780,261,000
11) 6,680,000,972,489
12) 38,167,245,907,567
13) 62,791,368,180,349
14) 9,726,354,808,346
15) 39,214,675,830,544

Day 82:
1) One hundred thirty-four trillion, eight hundred ninety billion, forty-three million, six hundred twenty-nine thousand, one hundred seventy
2) Four hundred forty-five trillion, six hundred seventy-eight billion, nine hundred one million, two hundred eighty-four thousand, six hundred fifty-seven
3) Eight hundred sixty-three trillion, two hundred forty-one billion, one hundred seventy-eight thousand, six hundred thirty
4) Twelve trillion, seven hundred sixty billion, three hundred ninety-eight million, eight hundred forty-six thousand, seven hundred forty-three
5) One trillion, sixty-three billion, five hundred eighteen million, four hundred nine thousand, two hundred eighty-one
6) Nine hundred fifty-six trillion, two hundred four billion, one hundred eighty-seven million, six hundred twenty-two thousand
7) Seventy-eight trillion, seven hundred fifty-four billion, three hundred twenty-one million, ninety-eight thousand two hundred sixty-eight
8) Five hundred eighty trillion, one hundred twenty-three billion, six hundred seventy-eight million, five hundred ninety-three thousand, four hundred nineteen
9) Twenty trillion, five hundred ninety-eight billion, seven hundred sixty-three million, four hundred seventy-one thousand, eight hundred five

Day 83:
1) 616,000,000,000,000, 615,760,000,000,000
2) 193,000,000,000,000, 192,840,000,000,000
3) 6,000,000,000,000, 5,710,000,000,000
4) 539,000,000,000,000, 538,620,000,000,000
5) 79,000,000,000,000, 79,300,000,000,000
6) 94,000,000,000,000, 93,870,000,000,000
7) 270,000,000,000,000, 270,490,000,000,000
8) 430,000,000,000,000, 429,920,000,000,000
9) 3,000,000,000,000, 3,160,000,000,000
10) 860,000,000,000,000, 860,230,000,000,000
11) 20,000,000,000,000, 19,830,000,000,000
12) 216,000,000,000,000, 216,360,000,000,000
13) 479,000,000,000,000, 479,050,000,000,000
14) 8,000,000,000,000, 7,910,000,000,000
15) 826,000,000,000,000, 826,300,000,000,000
16) 17,000,000,000,000, 17,280,000,000,000
17) 354,000,000,000,000, 354,170,000,000,000
18) 2,000,000,000,000, 1,650,000,000,000
19) 709,000,000,000,000, 709,270,000,000,000
20) 90,000,000,000,000, 90,460,000,000,000

Day 84:
1) 85.4 billion, eighty-five point four billion
2) 94.8 billion, ninety-four point eight billion
3) 64.3 billion, sixty-four point three billion
4) 36.9 billion, thirty-six point nine billion
5) 96.1 billion, ninety-six point one billion
6) 62.7 billion, sixty-two point seven billion
7) 30.5 billion, thirty point five billion
8) 42.8 billion, forty-two point eight billion
9) 78.2 billion, seventy-eight point two billion
10) 16 billion, sixteen billion
11) 43.5 billion, forty-three point five billion
12) 70.0 billion, seventy point zero billion
13) 19.3 billion, nineteen point three billion
14) 29.2 billion, twenty-nine point two billion
15) 57.9 billion, fifty-seven point nine billion
16) 27.8 billion, twenty-seven point eight billion
17) 51.2 billion, fifty-one point two billion
18) 89.1 billion, eighty-nine point one billion
19) 24.7 billion, twenty-four point seven billion
20) 81.7 billion, eighty-one point seven billion

Day 85:
1) 38.7 billion 2) 134.7 billion
3) 9.5 billion 4) 24.1 billion
5) 149.3 billion 6) 65.7 billion
7) 14 billion 8) 9.4 billion
9) 73.3 billion 10) 4.2 trillion
11) 14.5 trillion 12) 11.9 trillion
13) 6.1 trillion 14) 113 trillion
15) 7.4 trillion 16) 68.9 trillion
17) 13.9 trillion 18) 80.6 trillion

Day 86:
1) 9.2 billion 2) 81.7 billion
3) 10.3 billion 4) 52.4 billion
5) 39.1 billion 6) 103.9 billion
7) 20 billion 8) 118.9 billion
9) 88.2 billion 10) 157.4 trillion
11) 13.4 trillion 12) 56.7 trillion
13) 142.4 trillion 14) 22.6 trillion
15) 53.2 trillion 16) 16.6 trillion
17) 51.4 trillion 18) 18.2 trillion

© Libro Studio LLC 2020

Answers

Day 87:
1) 65.9 billion 2) 13 billion
3) 27.3 billion 4) 107.4 billion
5) 9 billion 6) 16.2 billion
7) 90.3 billion 8) 9.2 billion
9) 110.3 billion 10) 12.9 trillion
11) 100.5 trillion 12) 99.8 trillion
13) 30 trillion 14) 16.3 trillion
15) 84.1 trillion 16) 9.2 trillion
17) 94.1 trillion 18) 80.8 trillion

Day 88:
1) 0.2 billion 2) 38 billion
3) 4 billion 4) 2.6 billion
5) 87.1 billion 6) 71.5 billion
7) 3.4 billion 8) 45.8 billion
9) 13 billion 10) 5.3 trillion
11) 0.6 trillion 12) 6.5 trillion
13) 14.2 trillion 14) 21.9 trillion
15) 5.2 trillion 16) 57 trillion
17) 9.1 trillion 18) 32.6 trillion

Day 89:
1) 3.6 billion 2) 7.8 billion
3) 2.1 billion 4) 75.2 billion
5) 59.5 billion 6) 1.2 billion
7) 75.5 billion 8) 17.4 billion
9) 75.7 billion 10) 3.5 trillion
11) 32.3 trillion 12) 2.1 trillion
13) 63.9 trillion 14) 53.7 trillion
15) 64.9 trillion 16) 39 trillion
17) 6.8 trillion 18) 42.1 trillion

Day 90:
1) 74.2 billion 2) 78.2 billion
3) 21.3 billion 4) 60 billion
5) 76.9 billion 6) 106.8 billion
7) 137 trillion 8) 15.1 trillion
9) 58.3 trillion 10) 91.9 trillion
11) 114.7 trillion 12) 18.8 trillion

Day 91:
1) 40 minutes 2) 130 apples
3) 60 boys 4) 70 years

Day 92:
1) 500 chickens 2) 800 points
3) 2,100 people 4) 200 pages

Day 93:
1) 1,000 kg 2) 3,000 candies
3) 4,000 emails 4) 14,000 babies

Day 94:
1) 99,000 chairs 2) 15,000 website visitors
3) 3,000 pictures deleted 4) 15,000 coffees

Day 95:
1) 60,000 people live 2) 370,000 views
3) 80,000 tickets 4) 90,000 coins

Day 96:
1) 400,000 viewers 2) 500,000 plastic shopping bags
3) 900,000 people 4) 100,000 points

Day 97:
1) 11,000,000 people 2) 105,000,000 crayons
3) 5,000,000 crayons 4) 17,000,000 crayons

Day 98:
1) 3,100,000 cars 2) 41,700,000 people
3) 11,200,000,000 people 4) 1,600,000 tickets

Day 99:
1) 20 million people 2) 32 million trees
3) 17 million 4) 11 million items

Day 100:
1) 3 gigawatts 2) 41 gigabytes
3) 48 gigabytes 4) 5 seconds

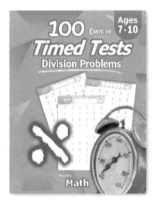
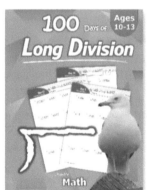

© Libro Studio LLC 2020

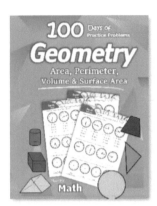   

Thank you moms, dads, and caregivers.
Thank you teachers and homeschooling parents.
Special thanks to all the helpful big brothers and sisters.
Ultimate thanks to the student. It's your effort that matters most!

Have questions, suggestions, or ideas for future resources?
Contact us at www.HumbleMath.com

© 2020, Libro Studio LLC. The purchase of this publication entitles the buyer to reproduce practice pages for classroom use only—not for commercial resale. Reproduction of this publication's material for an entire school or district is prohibited. No part of this book may be reproduced (except as noted above), transmitted in any form or by any means, electronic or mechanical, including photocopying, recording, or any other information storage and retrieval system, without the written permission of the publisher.

The Humble Math word mark is a trademark of Libro Studio LLC and is registered in the U.S. Patent and Trademark Office.

ISBN: 978-1-63578-331-5

Current contact information can be found at:
www.HumbleMath.com
www.LibroStudioLLC.com

Cover and title page image credit (turtle): BlueRingMedia/Shutterstock.com

Disclaimers:

The creator and publisher DO NOT GUARANTEE THE ACCURACY, RELIABILITY, OR COMPLETENESS OF THE CONTENT OF THIS BOOK OR RELATED RESOURSES AND IS NOT RESPONSIBLE FOR ANY ERRORS OR OMISSIONS. We apologize for any inaccurate, outdated, or misleading information. Feel free to contact us if you have questions or concerns.

Information in this book should not be considered advice nor treated as advice. ALWAYS SEEK ADVICE FROM A QUALIFIED PROFESSIONAL BEFORE MAKING DECISIONS BASED ON THE INFORMATION FOUND IN THIS BOOK OR RELATED RESOURCES. The creator and publisher are not liable for any decision made or action taken based on this book's content and information nor that of any related resource. You and any other persons are responsible for your own judgments, decisions, and actions.

Other resources, such as, but not limited to websites, videos, individuals, and organizations, may be referenced in this book or related resources but THIS DOES NOT MEAN THE CREATOR OR PUBLISHER ENDORSES THE INFORMATION THAT IS PROVIDED BY THESE RESOURCES. The creator and publisher of this book will not be liable for any information, claim, or recommendation obtained from these referenced resources. These referenced resources may also become outdated or unavailable. Websites, links, videos, and other resources may be changed, altered or removed over time.

This book and its contents are provided "AS IS" without warranty of any kind, expressed or implied, and hereby disclaims all implied warranties, including any warranty of merchantability and warranty of fitness for a particular purpose.

Libro Studio LLC publishes books and other content in a variety of print and electronic formats. Some content that appears in one format may not be available in other formats. For example, some content found in a print book may not be available in the eBook format, and vice versa. Furthermore, Libro Studio LLC reserves the right to update, alter, unpublish, and/or republish the content of any of these formats at any time.

© Libro Studio LLC 2020

Made in United States
Troutdale, OR
04/24/2024

19416144R00064